Latino Food Culture

Food Cultures in America
Ken Albala, General Editor

African American Food Culture
William Frank Mitchell

Asian American Food Culture
Jane E. Dusselier

Latino Food Culture
Zilkia Janer

Jewish American Food Culture
Jonathan Deutsch and Rachel D. Saks

Regional American Food Culture
Lucy M. Long

Latino Food Culture

ZILKIA JANER

Food Cultures in America

Ken Albala, General Editor

GREENWOOD PRESS
Westport, Connecticut • London

Library of Congress Cataloging-in-Publication Data

Janer, Zilkia.
  Latino food culture / Zilkia Janer.
    p. cm. — (Food cultures in America)
  Includes bibliographical references and index.
  ISBN-13: 978–0–313–34027–7 (alk. paper)
  ISBN-13: 978–0–313–34127–4 (set : alk. paper)
1. Cookery, Latin American.   2. Hispanic Americans—Food.
3. Hispanic Americans—Social life and customs.   4. Food habits—
United States. I. Title.
  TX716.A1J36   2008
  641.598—dc22   2007047969

British Library Cataloguing in Publication Data is available.

Library of Congress Catalog Card Number: 2007047969
ISBN: 978–0–313–34027–7 (vol.)
        978–0–313–34127–4 (set)

First published in 2008

Greenwood Press, 88 Post Road West, Westport, CT 06881
An imprint of Greenwood Publishing Group, Inc.
www.greenwood.com

Printed in the United States of America

The paper used in this book complies with the
Permanent Paper Standard issued by the National
Information Standards Organization (Z39.48–1984).

10 9 8 7 6 5 4 3 2 1

The publisher has done its best to make sure the instructions and/or recipes in this book
are correct. However, users should apply judgment and experience when preparing recipes,
especially parents and teachers working with young people. The publisher accepts no
responsibility for the outcome of any recipe included in this volume.

To my father, for teaching me how to appreciate bacalao, yuca, yautía, and ñame.
To my mother, for teaching me how to make sofrito.

Contents

Series Foreword

If you think of iconic and quintessentially American foods, those with which we are most familiar, there are scarcely any truly native to North America. Our hot dogs are an adaptation of sausages from Frankfurt and Vienna; our hamburgers are another Germanic import reconfigured. Ketchup is an invention of Southeast Asia, although it is based on the tomato, which comes from South America. Pizza is a variant on a Neapolitan dish. Colas are derived from an African nut. Our beloved peanuts are a South American plant brought to Africa and from there to the U.S. South. Our french fries are an Andean tuber, cooked with a European technique. Even our quintessentially American apple pie is made from a fruit native to what is today Kazakhstan.

When I poll my students about their favorite foods at the start of every food class I teach, inevitably included are tacos, bagels, sushi, pasta, fried chicken—most of which can be found easily at fast food outlets a few blocks from campus. In a word, American food culture is, and always has been profoundly globally oriented. This, of course, has been the direct result of immigration, from the time of earliest settlement by Spanish, English, French and Dutch, of slaves brought by force from Africa, and later by Germans, Italians, Eastern Europeans, including Jews, and Asians, up until now with the newest immigrants from Latin America and elsewhere.

Although Americans have willingly adopted the foods of newcomers, we never became a "melting pot" for these various cultures. So-called ethnic cuisines naturally changed on foreign soil, adapting to new ingredients and popular taste—but at heart they remain clear and proud descendants of their respective countries. Their origins are also readily recognized by Americans;

we are all perfectly familiar with the repertoire of Mexican, Chinese, and Italian restaurants, and increasingly now Thai, Japanese, and Salvadoran, to name a few. Eating out at such restaurants is a hallmark of mainstream American culture, and despite the spontaneous or contrived fusion of culinary styles, each retains its unique identity.

This series is designed as an introduction to the major food cultures of the United States. Each volume delves deeply into the history and development of a distinct ethnic or regional cuisine. The volumes further explore these cuisines through their major ingredients, who is cooking and how at home, the structure of mealtime and daily rituals surrounding food, and the typical meals and how they are served, which can be dramatically different from popular versions. In addition, chapters cover eating out, holidays and special occasions, as well as the influence of religion, and the effect of the diet on health and nutrition. Recipes are interspersed throughout. Each volume offers valuable features including a timeline, glossary and index, making each a convenient reference work for research.

The importance of this series for our understanding of ourselves is several-fold. Food is so central to how we define ourselves, so in a sense this series will not only recount how recipes and foodways serve as distinct reminders of ethnic identity, binding families and communities together through shared experiences, but it also describes who we have all become, since each food culture has become an indispensable part of our collective identity as Americans.

Ken Albala
General Editor

Acknowledgments

I am grateful to the family, friends, and colleagues that made writing this book pleasurable and enlightening. My parents Edda Vila and Pedro A. Janer patiently answered all kinds of questions regarding Puerto Rican culture. My friends Pepa Anastasio, Mario Bick, Diana Brown, Brenda Elsey, Jeffrey Harris, Svetlana Mintcheva, Kalpana Raina, William Rubel, Benita Sampedro, and Frederique Thiollet were always willing to try and discuss Latino food with me at home and in restaurants. Private conversations and the published work of Arlene Dávila, Luis Duno-Gottberg, Lázaro Lima, and Walter Mignolo enabled me to understand and explain Latino food culture in the broader context of Latina/o cultural politics. I am grateful to my colleagues at Hofstra University for understanding that the study of food is a serious and necessary academic endeavor, and to my Latina/o students for sharing their knowledge and experience of Latino culinary culture. This book was written in the Frederick Lewis Allen Research Study Room of the New York Public Library, where the daily company of fellow writers Maggie Jackson and Mark Lamster was energizing even on the days when we did not exchange a single word. Ken Albala and Wendi Schnaufer at Greenwood Press provided unobtrusive guidance. I finally thank Sanjib Baruah for his unmatched wit, enthusiasm, and palate.

Introduction

Lilo González, a Salvadoran artist living in Washington, D.C., sings a song called "*Forjando un solo pueblo*" ("Forging a Single People") in which he describes wanting to have a big party, with iconic foods from Latin America: tacos from México, *pupusas* from El Salvador, *arepas* fromVenezuela, and roasted pig. Latinos come from many different national, ethnic, and socioeconomic backgrounds but most face similar problems of poverty, discrimination, and racism in the United States. To help change this situation, in the song González calls for unity to form one single transnational Latino community. His call for solidarity is expressed in the language of food, a realm in which the creation of a transnational Latino culture is already apparent.

Tacos, *pupusas,* and *arepas* are only a few of the many delicious foods with which Latinos have enriched the cuisine of the United States. Aside from the dishes that they have brought from their home countries and the ones that they have adapted, improvised, and created in the United States, the important role of Latinos in the food system of the United States cannot be overestimated. Most of the food consumed in this country is either grown, harvested, processed, cooked, or served by Latinos. Whether as inheritors and creators of sophisticated cuisines, or as the workforce that sustains the food system from the fields to the table, Latinos are a vital force in the food culture of the United States.

The 2000 U.S. Census indicates that Latinos constitute 12.5 percent of the population. There is a misconception that all Latinos are recent immigrants, but Latinos have been in the territory of the United States before the United States came into existence. Considering that many Latinos in the Southwest are descendants of the indigenous peoples that inhabited the region before the arrival of Europeans, that the first Europeans to explore and found settlements in the territory were from Spain, that much of the U.S. Southwest was a part of México, and that all Puerto Ricans are U.S. citizens, it becomes obvious that Latino and Anglo Americans have a long common history. The Mexican American War in 1848, the Spanish American War in 1898, the many U.S. interventions in Latin America during the Cold War, and the violence and displacements provoked by the Central American civil wars from the late 1970s to early 1990s and the current U.S.-backed drug war, all in great part account for the growth of the Latino population in the form of documented and undocumented immigrants, refugees, and exiles.

The category *Latino* is a construct created in the United States to refer to the highly heterogeneous people that live in the United States and whose immediate or distant origins can be traced to Spanish- and Portuguese-speaking Latin American and Caribbean countries. The U.S. government uses the term *Hispanic* to refer to the same people (excluding Brazilians because they speak Portuguese and *Hispanic* refers to Spain and the Spanish language), and categories like *Latin* or even *Spanish* are also widely used. There is much debate regarding which term to use, since all these words in one way or another privilege the Spanish element of a group that contains multiple kinds and combinations of Amerindian, African, European, and Asian peoples. The word *Latino* (which strictly speaking refers to everybody who speaks a language derived from Latin) does not really solve this problem, but since it is a term of self-affirmation, as opposed to a government imposition, it is the preferred term in this book.

Another issue is whether a single term can be used to refer to so many different peoples. Many Latinos prefer to refer to themselves with national terms like *Mexican* or *Puerto Rican* as people generally do in Latin America. This is not only the result of the nationalism of 20 different countries (Argentina, Bolivia, Brazil, Chile, Colombia, Costa Rica, Cuba, Dominican Republic, Ecuador, El Salvador, Guatemala, Honduras, México, Nicaragua, Panamá, Paraguay, Perú, Puerto Rico, Uruguay, and Venezuela), it also reflects the fact that each of these countries is multiethnic in different ways. For example, in México the majority of the population is constituted by dozens of different Amerindian ethnic groups, Spanish and other European descendants, and *Mestizos* that have resulted from the mix of Amerindians and Europeans. In Puerto Rico, Cuba, and the Dominican Republic, people have mostly mixed Spanish and African ancestry, whereas in Argentina the dominant ancestry is European. Many people question how a single category can possibly include a Maya Amerindian from Guatemala, a rural *Mestizo* from México, a white urban Argentinean, and an Afro Puerto Rican.

Another element that accounts for Latino heterogeneity is related to migration patterns. There are significant differences depending on when, where, and under what circumstances a group migrated. Can a Cuban entrepreneur who received political asylum and settled in Miami's Little Havana, a third-generation Mexican American studying in Los Angeles, a Guatemalan migrant farm worker in North Carolina, and an undocumented Peruvian in New York City all be considered part of the same group? On the one hand, it seems as unthinkable as calling all English-speaking people living in France "English" whether they came from India, England, Hong Kong, or the United States. On the other hand, even though a significant number of Latinos do not speak Spanish, there is no doubt that the language serves as a connecting thread both in the way in which Latinos are perceived by mainstream U.S. society and in the way in which they interact with each other in the U.S. context. *Latino* is a pliable identity that has been in the making in the United States for more than one century as a process of imposition, contestation, and negotiation.

Chronology

1845   Texas is annexed to the United States.

1848   The Treaty of Guadalupe Hidalgo puts an end to the Mexican American War, transforming 55 percent of the Mexican territory into present-day Arizona, California, New México, and parts of Colorado, Nevada, and Utah.

1893   The Texas exhibit at the Columbian Exhibition in Chicago begins to spread the popularity of the Tex-Mex cuisine that Mexicans had created to cater to Anglo customers in Texas.

1898   Cuba and Puerto Rico become colonies of the United States as a result of the Treaty of Paris that puts an end to the Spanish American War.

       Encarnación Pinedo publishes *El cocinero español (The Spanish Cook)*, California's first Spanish-language cookbook.

ca. 1900 Chili powder—a mix of ground chiles, cumin, oregano, and black pepper—is invented in the Southwest as a shortcut for cooking Mexican-style dishes and becomes the signature of Tex-Mex cooking.

1910–1930 The Mexican Revolution fuels the massive migration of an estimated 1.5 million Mexicans to the United States.

1917	Puerto Rico becomes a territory of the United States and Puerto Ricans are given a limited U.S. citizenship.
1920s	Puerto Ricans own hundreds of restaurants and *bodegas* (stores) in New York City.
1936	Prudencio Unanue founds Goya Foods, the largest Latino-owned food company in the United States.
	The covered food market nicknamed "La Marqueta" opens in New York City, providing hard-to-find foods like salted codfish, plantains, and root vegetables.
1940s–1950s	Cubans own several restaurants, butcher shops, and grocery stores in New York City.
1952	Puerto Rico becomes a Commonwealth or *Estado Libre Asociado* of the United States. Massive migration of Puerto Ricans to New York, New Jersey, and Florida follows.
1959	The Cuban Revolution causes the massive migration of Cubans who transform Miami Dade County of Florida into a Little Havana.
1960s	Taco Bell and Taco Maker start the fast-food version of Mexican food catering to non-Mexican customers.
1962	César Chávez launches the National Farm Workers Association. Many other Chicano, Nuyorican, and Latino civil rights organizations emerge in this period.
1965	The United States invades the Dominican Republic. Dominican migrants start to settle in New York in larger numbers.
1970s–1980s	Political turmoil in Central American countries sparks immigration in the form of refugees and undocumented migrants. Central Americans start to widen the repertoire of Latin American foods and ingredients available in the United States.
1972	Diana Kennedy publishes the cookbook *The Cuisines of Mexico*, in which she invites readers to realize that Tex-Mex cuisine is a far cry from the rich diversity of Mexican cuisines.
1978	The first Calle Ocho Festival is held Miami. It has become a large street party that attracts more than 1 million people and features hundreds of Latino food kiosks.

1980s	South American immigration starts to grow, completing the representation of all Latin American countries in the development of Latino food culture.
1990s	*Nuevo Latino*, the upscale version of pan-Latino cuisine, grows in popularity as restaurants multiply.
1994	The North American Free Trade Agreement begins, gradually eliminating barriers to agricultural trade between México and the United States.
2003	Latinos become the largest minority group in the United States.
	Nuevo Latino chef Aaron Sánchez publishes *La comida del barrio*, a cookbook featuring the foods of Latino East Harlem, New York.
2007	*Gourmet* magazine publishes a special collector's issue, "Latino Food: America's Fastest Rising Cuisine," recognizing the wide national and regional diversity of Latino cuisines.
	Guatemalan fast-food chain *Pollo Campero* has 35 restaurants all over the United States.
	Latino chefs Daisy Martínez and Ingrid Hoffmann host national television cooking shows.

1

Historical Overview

MEXICAN AMERICAN CUISINE

People of Mexican origin or heritage are both the largest Latino group and the one with the longest common history with the United States. The cultural continuity between the two sides of the México–United States border predates the arrival of Europeans and the birth of both countries.

2600 B.C. to A.D. 1521: Mesoamerican Culinary Cultures from the Domestication of Maize to the Fall of Tenochtitlan

The base of Mexican American cuisine was laid by the people that domesticated *maize* (the indigenous name of corn) in southern México about 4,600 years ago. Many different ethnic groups constituted the Aztec empire in central México and the Maya empire in southern México and Central America. They were two of the most advanced civilizations in the Western Hemisphere. Mesoamerican architecture, science, and arts were highly developed and Tenochtitlan, today's México City, was probably the largest city in the world when the Europeans arrived in the fifteenth century. The markets in Tenochtitlan astonished the Spanish newcomers because of the variety of ingredients and prepared foods available. The royal cuisine of the Aztecs and the Mayas benefited from goods and cultural expertise from all over the vast empires, resulting in an extremely varied and complex cuisine.

Aztec and Mayan cuisines were based on maize. Around 1200–1500 B.C., they developed the process of *nixtamalization*, which consists on cooking and soaking dry maize kernels in an alkaline slaked lime solution to make the grain easier to grind. The process also makes the protein and vitamin contents of maize easier to absorb by the human body. This lime-processed ground maize, called *nixtamal*, is ground to make the *masa* (dough) for tortillas, tamales, and many other dishes. *Nixtamalization* is essential for maize to provide adequate nutrition but Europeans did not adopt the procedure. The dependence on maize without *nixtamalization* as a main staple in part accounts for the outbreaks of pellagra—a disease caused by vitamin B niacin deficiency—that plagued the peasant population of Europe for centuries.

The importance of maize as the staple that provided sustenance for the creation of Aztec and Maya civilizations is highlighted in its cultural and religious significance. Mayan creation stories indicate that the gods created mankind from maize, so the plant is respected as life itself. The importance of maize in Mesoamerican culture is parallel to the importance of wheat in European cuisines and religions. Wheat has been the most important staple in European history and, in the form of bread, it remains at the center of the Eucharist rite in which it represents or becomes the body of Christ.

Beans, chiles, vanilla, chocolate, tomatoes, avocados, squash, and numerous fruits are only the most notorious of the wealth of ingredients that originated in Mesoamerica, and all of them are still essential to Latin American and Latino cuisines. The combination of maize and beans constitutes a complete protein that made Amerindian cuisines as nutritious as those based on animal protein. Turkey and other small animals were available and eaten before the arrival of Europeans, but animal flesh was not an important component of Mesoamerican cuisines until the Spanish introduced pork and cattle. The abundance and variety of ingredients available to Mayan and Aztec peoples was surpassed only by the diversity of dishes that were prepared with them. The Spanish Friar Bernardino de Sahagún in the sixteenth century commented on the many kinds of chiles, tortillas, *moles* (complex sauces made with ground chiles and spices), and tamales available in the Aztec market. This is how he described some of the foods offered by a tortilla vendor:

He sells tamales, turkey pasties, plain tamales, barbecued tamales, those cooked in an olla—they burn within; grains of maize with chili, tamales with chili, burning within; fish tamales, fish with grains of maize, axolotl tamales, tadpoles with grains of maize, mushrooms with grains of maize, tuna cactus with grains of maize, rabbit tamales, rabbit with grains of maize, gopher tamales: tasty—tasty, very tasty, very well made, always tasty, savory, of pleasing odor, of very pleasing odor; made with a pleasing odor, very savory. Where [it is] tasty, [it has] chili, salt, tomatoes, gourd seeds: shredded, crumbled, juiced.[1]

Sahagún also described at length the luxurious multicourse meals served to the nobility, which included an assortment of tortillas, tamales, *moles*, fruits, *atoles* (maize meal drinks), fowl and fish stews, and which culminated with many different cacao drinks.[2]

By the time the Spanish arrived, the process of nixtamalization to make *masa* for tortillas and tamales and the cultivation of the key foods that were domesticated in Mesoamerica—maize, chiles, beans, and squash—had gradually reached the region of contemporary northern México and of the contemporary Southwest of the United States. This region was inhabited by nonsedentary groups like the Seri in the present territory of California and in the Mexican state of Sonora, and by sedentary peoples like the Pecos, Zuni, and other Pueblo villages along the Río Grande and the Little Colorado and Pecos Rivers. However, the majority of Amerindians in the Southwest were semisedentary groups that supplemented maize agriculture with deer and other game hunting, and with desert plants like prickly pear, maguey, and mesquite beans. The Spanish called them *ranchería* people and they comprised the Tarahumara, Conchos, Yaqui, Mayo, Lower Pima, Upper Pima, Opata, Yuma, and the Tohono O'odham.[3] Amerindian food in the Southwest was not as elaborate as in Mesoamerica due in part to the more limited availability of fruits and vegetables in arid areas and to the relatively smaller and simpler social organization. The cuisine of the frontier region has always been related to but different from the cuisine of central México.

1521–1821: Spanish Colonial Period to Mexican Independence

The Spanish colonial period in México stretches from 1521 with the fall of the city of Tenochtitlan until the declaration of independence 300 years later. The Spanish renamed the territory "Viceroyalty of New Spain" and established a centralized colonial government on the same site as the destroyed Aztec capital city. They instituted a highly hierarchized social order organized around the idea of race and blood purity. At the top of the hierarchy were the Spanish that were born in Spain, followed by *Criollos* (Spaniards born in the New Spain). At the lower end were the *Mestizos* (mixed Spanish and Amerindians), while Amerindians were at the bottom. The Spanish exploited the organization and skills of Amerindians, forcing them to work for them in the fields and in the mines. The colonial institution called *encomienda* granted authority to the Spanish to enslave Amerindians and to forcefully convert them to Christianity. Aztec and Maya peoples were reduced to slavery and the status and quality of their cuisine also suffered.

The racial hierarchies created by Europeans to justify the subordination and exploitation of Amerindians also assigned an inferior status to their cuisine. The colonizing mission depended on military power as well as on the imposition of Spanish culture and categories of knowledge. The project of religious and cultural conversion was extended to the kitchen. Great efforts were made to make the Amerindian population change from their maize-based diet to the wheat-based diet of Europe. This campaign was only partially successful and was embraced mostly by *Criollos* and upper-class *Mestizos*, and has had its ups and downs throughout Mexican history.

The Spanish brought many ingredients from Europe, Asia, and Africa like lentils, chickpeas, citrus fruits, onions, garlic, rice, sugar, bananas, and eggplants. They also introduced cheese-making and meat-curing techniques. The Spanish were fond of meat and lard, so meat became more available as they dedicated to livestock many of the fields that were previously used for maize cultivation. Lard became a part of the *masa* (*nixtamalized* maize dough) for tortillas and tamales, and meat was added to many Amerindian dishes. Ingredients and techniques from Spain and Mesoamerica gradually blended to create a distinctly Mexican cuisine with many regional variations.

Shortly after Mexican independence many cookbooks were published, including the three-volume *El cocinero mexicano (The Mexican Cook)* published in 1831. *Mestizos* and Amerindians in the villages kept their food habits relatively close to regional precolonial ways, while urban *Criollos* and *Mestizos* developed a more mixed and cosmopolitan cuisine. This cookbook shows that the Mexican upper classes felt equally comfortable with European and Amerindian cuisines and had made them their own. The organization of the cookbook is similar to the standard format of nineteenth-century European cookbooks, including one full volume devoted to meat, fowl, and seafood, and another one dedicated to sweets, cakes, and pastries. The first volume includes a variety of chapters including stocks, sauces, and the unusual category "light lunches," which contains maize and chile-based dishes. The fact that Amerindian dishes were included—but segregated—is indicative of the subordinate role that Amerindians had in the new *Criollo* and *Mestizo* nation. The cookbook shows Amerindian influence throughout all chapters in the use of Mesoamerican ingredients and techniques to prepare European dishes, but it obscures the fact that Amerindian cuisines are complex and varied enough to fill many volumes by themselves. In recent years there have been many efforts to document the incredible diversity of Mexican cuisines, including the 54-volume cookbook collection of indigenous and popular cuisines published by the Mexican National Council for Culture and the Arts (CONACULTA).

Mexican cuisine developed with significant regional differences based on ethnic and geographical diversity. Six general gastronomic areas have been identified: the Pacific coast, western México, central México, the isthmus of Tehuantepec, the Mayan area, and northern México. The Pacific coast is distinguished by fish and seafood dishes, whereas western México is characterized by hot and spicy dishes like thick meat-based soups called *birria, pozole,* and *menudo,* and by enchiladas, tostadas, and gorditas. Central México includes the sophisticated cuisine of Puebla represented by *mole poblano* (turkey cooked in a complex sauce that blends spices, chocolate, and chiles), *chiles en nogada* (poblano peppers stuffed with meat, nuts, and candied fruits), and *pipián* (a fricassee made with ground pumpkin seeds and chiles), and the cosmopolitan cuisine of México City better known for tortilla soup and *budín azteca* (a casserole made of layered tortillas, vegetables, chicken, sauce, and cheese). The isthmus of Tehuantepec shows a strong Amerindian culinary influence best exemplified by the state of Oaxaca, known as the "land of the seven moles." The Maya area includes the Yucatán peninsula and it is distinguished by its variety of tamales and *masa*-based snacks, and by dishes like *papadzules* (tacos with pumpkin seed sauce) and *cochinita pibil* (pork marinated in annatto and bitter orange, and barbecued in banana leaves). The cuisine of northern México is distinguished by the abundance of beef dishes, by the use of wheat flour tortillas, and by a stringy local cheese called Chihuahua. Some of the favorite dishes of northern México are *sopaipillas* (fried pieces of wheat flour tortillas), chimichangas, *pozole* (hominy stew), and roast kid.[4] This mild, hearty, and relatively simple frontier cuisine of northern México is the base of Mexican and Mexican American cuisines in the U.S. Southwest.

During Spanish rule, the frontier region developed differently from the rest of México as it is still reflected in its food culture. The Spanish did not give the frontier region the same attention that they gave to the richer and more highly populated central areas. The settlers who came after the end of the sixteenth century had been introduced to many forms of Amerindian cooking in the Mexican plateau, but once they became isolated in the northern provinces they relied largely on traditional Spanish cooking.[5] This explains the preference for wheat flour tortillas and for less spicy dishes.

The Spanish colonization of the northern frontier of the New Spain was performed through the establishment of *presidios* and *misiones* (missions). *Presidios* were military fortresses used to defend the territory, and missions were monastic institutions in which the mostly semisedentary Amerindians of the region were Christianized and forced to work. The societies established by the missions were stratified based on different levels of assimilation of Christian religion and culture. The colonists gave privileges to the Christianized Amerindians who lived in the missions (called *neophytes*) over the nonmission Amerindians who worked on the ranches (called *gentiles*). Amerindians worked on the missions around the clock as they produced the grains, vegetables, fruit, meat, cloth, clothing, and leather goods that were distributed by the mission housekeeper to the military troops, the missionaries, their servants, and the neophytes.[6] The testimonial of Eulalia Pérez, who was the housekeeper of the wealthy San Gabriel mission in the early nineteenth century, shows how food was used to mark rank differences. The mission produced olive oil and wine, and Eulalia and her daughters made chocolate, sweets, and lemonade. Many of Eulalia's delicacies were so highly esteemed that they were exported to Spain. The food ration for the troops and for the neophyte servants included beans, maize, chickpeas, lentils, and lard. In spite of the abundance and variety of foods available, Amerindians were fed a very limited diet served in separate quarters. Their breakfast was *pozole* (hominy stew) and meat on regular days, and *champurrado* (*atole* with chocolate) with bread and sweets only on festive occasions. For lunch they were served *pozole* with meat and vegetables, and for supper they had *atole* plain or with meat.

After Mexican independence in 1821 the missions and *presidios* were secularized and replaced by civil structures and militias.[7] Amerindians were emancipated and granted citizenship but continued their subordinate position as workers in the *ranchos*. The *rancheros* became the dominant class in this process of secularization and privatization of the lands. The food culture of the *rancheros* was the result of the history and the ecology of the frontier region. In New México, Arizona, and southwest Texas preservation by drying was a necessity, so they dried beef, fruits, and vegetables. Goats were introduced in semiarid areas that had few cattle. They provided milk for cheese, and roasted kid became a favorite food. In south Texas and California there was abundant forage for cattle to roam and reproduce. Beef was plentiful and cow's milk was used as a drink and to make *cuajada* (strained curds), butter, sour cream, cottage cheese, and *queso asadero* (a melting cheese used in dishes like *chile con queso*). Pork was used all over the region to make *chicharrones* (pork cracklings), *morcillas* (blood sausages), and *chorizo*. Pork was also marinated in *adobo* (made with vinegar, wine, garlic, red chiles, and spices) and cooked on a grill. *Rancheros* in Texas favored cooking sides of beef, pork, or mutton in *barbacoa*, a technique that the Spanish learned form the Amerindians of the Caribbean and Central America. They wrapped the meat in banana leaves, buried it in a pit, and topped it with large preheated rocks to roast it. Mexican *rancheros* adapted many Amerindian maize dishes like *menudo* (a stew of corn with beef viscera), *pozole* (a stew of corn made with pig's knuckles), and *chacales* (dried parboiled corn on the cob cooked with any meat), as well as the better-known tortillas, tacos, enchiladas, chalupas, tostadas, and tamales. They also adapted dishes from Spain like *sopaipillas*, *buñuelos* (fried egg-rich dough spiced with cinnamon and cloves), and *bizcochitos* (small flat cookies). The cuisine was based on ranching and subsistence agriculture and those who could afford it imported luxury items like brandy, chocolate, and coffee.[8]

Nixtamal for Pozole

(Note: These ingredients can be found in Mexican shops.)

1 cup dried white   1 TBSP cal (slaked lime)
   cacahuazintle maize   4 cups water

Wash the maize under running water. Heat the water in a large noncorrosive pan over high heat and add *cal*, stirring until it dissolves. Add the maize to the pan and remove any floating kernels. Bring the water to a boil. Reduce the heat to medium and simmer for 15 minutes. Remove the pan from the heat and let the maize soak for 15 minutes. In a colander, wash the maize thoroughly under running water to remove all traces of *cal*. Rub the kernels between your fingers to remove the remaining skin particles until all the kernels are white. Pick off the little brown heads of each kernel if you want them to open fully when boiled. Boil the maize in plenty of unsalted water until soft, 3 to 4 hours. Drain and use in any *pozole* stew recipe.

Note: Instead of boiling the maize a second time, this nixtamalized maize can be soaked for 1 hour and ground to make fresh *masa* (dough) for tamales. To make *masa* for tortillas the maize is boiled for only 2 minutes and soaked overnight before grinding.

Pozole Stew

2 TBSP vegetable oil
1 pound pork ribs or any
   other pork meat with bones
1 onion, chopped
2–3 cloves garlic, minced
4 cups water

2 cups freshly prepared
   nixtamal, or 1 15-ounce
   can white hominy
1 dry *guajillo* chile
1 dry *ancho* chile
Salt

For the garnish:
1 TBSP dried Mexican oregano
2 limes, cut into quarters
1 small onion, chopped
1/2 cup cilantro, chopped

3 radishes, thinly sliced
1/4 small head of cabbage or
   iceberg lettuce, very thinly
   sliced

Split open the chiles, discarding the seeds and veins. In a heavy skillet over medium heat roast the chiles for a few seconds on both sides until blistered.

(continued)

Break them into small pieces and soak in hot water for 30 minutes. Grind in a mortar and pestle or blender, adding water as necessary to form a paste. Heat the oil over medium-high heat in a heavy-bottomed pot and sauté the onions, garlic, and meat for 20 minutes. Add the water, chile paste, and freshly made drained nixtamal (or drained and rinsed can of hominy) and simmer partially covered for 30–40 minutes. Remove the meat from the bones and cut into bite-sized pieces. Discard the bones and return the meat to the pot. Season to taste with salt and pepper. Serve the garnishes in small bowls, allowing people to choose their own combinations. Serves 6.

1846–1930: Mexican American War to Mexican Revolution

Between 1846 and 1848 the United States and México fought a war that was the culmination of the conflict between the weak Mexican government in the northern region and the expansionist ambitions of the United States. México lost the war and the Treaty of Guadalupe Hidalgo stipulated that México would surrender half of its national territory. The surrendered lands became the U.S. states of California, Texas, New México, Arizona, and parts of Colorado, Nevada, and Utah. The Río Bravo (called Rio Grande in the United States) was established as the definite border between the two countries. The Mexicans that lived in the new U.S. territory were allowed to stay and they were promised that their rights and property would be respected, but the overwhelming majority lost their lands. They also suffered from racist violence.

Mexican Latino cuisine in the U.S. Southwest developed in this tumultuous context in which Mexicans were dispossessed. Their food culture had to be adapted to poorer economic conditions and to the taste demands of the more powerful Anglo settlers. The same racist colonial logic used by the Spanish to classify Amerindian cuisines as inferior was used by Anglo Americans at this time to decide that the food of Mexicans was substandard. Mexican food—Spanish, *Mestizo*, and Amerindian alike—was considered unfit for human consumption as it symbolized the supposedly degenerate and despicable conquered Mexican population.[9] This attitude continued into the early twentieth century, when dieticians considered most traditional immigrant foods unhealthy. They tried to convince Mexicans to reduce their use of tomato and pepper, thinking that a blander dish would be easier to digest.[10]

The loss of wealth and status of Mexicans in the new sociopolitical context affected their cuisine. The elaborate and cosmopolitan cuisine of the Mexican elites had little opportunity of continuity and development. The case of Encarnación Pinedo, a member of a prominent Californio family that was among the earliest settlers of northern California, illustrates this loss. By 1856, eight members of Encarnación Pinedo's family had been lynched or shot by Yankee miners and vigilantes. Her family also lost their 160,000 acres of land in the Santa Clara valley.[11] Encarnación Pinedo's life had changed dramatically and she knew that the culture and way of life that she represented would soon be only a memory. In 1898 she published a testimony in the form of a cookbook: El cocinero español (The Spanish Cook), the first Spanish-language cookbook published in California. The fact that she called the book Spanish and not Mexican can be explained as a strategy of elite Californios to escape the racist disdain with which Mexicans were treated and to try to pass as second-class whites.[12] This was not just her personal strategy; it was consistent with the identity that Criollos and upper-class Mestizos had built for themselves all over Latin America after independence. Latin American elites used their European ancestry and education as a way to justify their continued dominance over Amerindians and, as they faced the rise of U.S. imperialism, they stressed the Spanishness of their nations in an effort to be respected as members of the Latin civilizations that have their origin in ancient Rome. Pinedo used this strategy in the introduction to her book by inserting her cooking in the history of culinary development from Persia and Greece to France and Italy.[13] Her selection of recipes is similar to El cocinero mexicano. It contains Spanish, Amerindian, and Mexican recipes together with the repertoire that was usually found in European cookbooks.

Another example of a Mexican woman who used her cooking as a bastion to protect her identity and her dignity as a Mexican in California was Delfina Valle. Valle came from Guadalajara to Los Angeles in 1926. Her new disadvantaged situation required that she worked and cooked, two activities for which she used to have domestic help in México. Shortage of money, time, and fresh ingredients made it impossible for her to cook the refined recipes that she brought with her from México. Still she managed to reproduce her cooking with improvisations and substitutions, and her family and fellow workers were devoted to her food, tired of the Anglo American foods that they were served by their employers.[14] Encarnación Pinedo and Valle's cooking was the cosmopolitan Mexican cooking that benefited from many Amerindian and European influences, but it was less practiced and relatively unknown in the United States compared to the food of working-class Mexicans in Texas.

The plaza in San Antonio, Texas, in 1895 has been described as similar to those in north México. Food sellers served tamales, tortillas, chiles rellenos (stuffed chiles), huevos revueltos (scrambled eggs), lengua lampreada (beef tongue with salsa ranchera), pucheros (soups), and ollas (stews). The difference was that in San Antonio Mexican food was enjoyed not only by Mexicans but also by Anglo Americans, Europeans, and African Americans.

Nineteenth-century travelers along the Southwestern frontier encountered Mexican food in outdoor neighborhood dining provided by Mexican families. By the early twentieth century Mexican restaurants were already advertised in tourist guides.[15]

Based on northern Mexican cooking, two different kinds of Mexican restaurant cuisines developed together: one that catered to Mexicans and another that catered to Anglo Americans. While the former strived to continue the food habits of generations, the latter became what is known as "Tex-Mex." Mexican restaurants that catered to Anglos served Mexican food prepared by Mexicans but the owners and the clientele were almost exclusively Anglo American. Just like the *chile colorado* (a red enchilada sauce) sold in outdoor food stands became "chili con carne" with the addition of plentiful amounts of meat, Mexican restaurant food became synonymous with the combination plate in which enchiladas or tamales are served with rice and refried beans and covered with melted cheese. The variety and subtlety of Mexican dishes that were typically enjoyed separately was reduced to one plate. The invention of chili powder (a mix of ground chiles, cumin, oregano, and black pepper) in the late 1890s further advanced the simplification of Mexican cuisine in the United States. Restaurants that catered to Anglos used chili powder instead of freshly ground chiles and spices, and used a "chili gravy" (a flour-based brown sauce with a little bit of chili powder) instead of the chile-based enchilada sauces that were too hot for the Anglo American palate.[16] Mexicans cooked this kind of food exclusively for their Anglo customers,

Chili con carne tables, San Antonio, Texas, circa 1865–1880. Photography Collection, Miriam and Ira D. Wallach Division of Art, Prints and Photographs, The New York Public Library, Astor, Lenox and Tilden Foundations.

and cooked in the traditional way at home and at restaurants that catered to Mexicans.

Between 1910 and 1930, because of the convulsions of the Mexican Revolution, about 1.5 million Mexicans migrated to the United States and settled mostly in Texas. Segregation laws were unofficially applied to Mexicans and Mexican Americans, creating enclave neighborhoods. In these enclaves, food stalls and restaurants catering to immigrants provided home-style food and served as community centers. The constant stream of immigrants coming from different parts of México revitalized Mexican American cuisine by bringing a fresh demand and supply of traditional regional cooking.

1930s–2007: Great Depression to Today

During the Great Depression as many as 1 million Mexicans and Mexican Americans from Arizona, Texas, and California were deported to México, including many that were U.S. citizens by birth. But in spite of anti-immigrant agitations, the need for workers prompted the U.S. government to continue a series of programs that would bring in hundreds of thousands of Mexican migrant farm workers. Exploitative low wages and the use of toxic chemicals on the fields and on the workers pushed farm workers to organize and conduct numerous strikes, marches, and boycotts. In the 1960s the Chicano or Mexican American Civil Rights Movement galvanized the Mexican and Mexican American population to defend farm workers rights, and in favor of enhanced voting, education, and political rights. The Chicano movement also fostered a resurgence of Mexican cultural pride that had its culinary expression in the flowering of Mexican food stands and *taquerías* (taco shops).

Today the Mexican American cuisine of the Southwest is considered the oldest regional cuisine of the United States. Southwestern cuisine extends throughout northern México, California, Arizona, and New México with the following variations: California Southwestern cuisine, distinguished by the use of avocado, sprouts, and sour cream; Arizona or Sonoran style that uses cactus fruits and incorporates Native American influences like fry bread; New Mexican or Santa Fe cuisine that emphasizes green chiles, blue corn, and *pozole*; and Tex-Mex, characterized by chili con carne, nachos, and barbecue.[17] While some experts see Southwestern cuisine as a bridge between Mexican American and Anglo American mainstream cultures, others are more critical. Some consider Southwestern cuisine, particularly in trend-setting restaurants, as an example of a hidden gastronomic culture war. It has been argued that the social relations of restaurant production that keeps Mexicans and Mexican Americans in lower-level positions, and the representation of Mexican cuisine as evocative of the conquered frontier, normalize the commercial and aesthetic appropriation of Mexican culture.[18]

Indeed, Mexicans and Mexican Americans have not been the main beneficiaries of the growing Mexican food industry, even though it depends on their labor and cultural expertise. Mexican restaurants and food distribution companies that serve a Mexican and Mexican American clientele are small-to medium-scale operations, whereas large scale operations at the national level are generally owned by Anglo Americans and big corporations. The first fast-food chains to mass market Mexican American food were Taco Maker and Taco Bell in the 1960s. Their version of the cuisine is so far removed from the way Mexican Latinos actually eat that the companies report that they constitute a negligible part of their clientele. Newer Mexican fast-food chains like Chipotle Mexican Grill and Tijuana Flats are not Latino-owned either. Even successful companies that originated in México, like snack foods producer Sabritas and tequila producer Casa Herradura, have been bought by bigger U.S. companies. Increasingly large supermarket chains like Fiesta Mart and even Wal-Mart are competing with neighborhood stores by focusing on Mexican and other Latino foods.

There is much more to Mexican American food culture than fast food and Southwestern cuisine. The regional cuisines of México in all their complexity can be found in Mexican and Mexican American homes and in restaurants, *taquerías*, *panaderías* (bakeries), and *mercados* (markets) all over the United States. Highway 1 between Los Angeles and San Francisco has recently been called "the hottest taco crawl outside of México" because of the large quantity and excellent quality of Mexican food available.[19] Even in New York City, a place historically associated with Caribbean Latinos rather than with Mexican Americans, a relatively recent wave of immigration from Puebla and Oaxaca has made available delicacies like *mole poblano* and *mole negro*, showing a face of Mexican cuisine that had been obscured by combination plates and burritos.

CARIBBEAN LATINO CUISINES

Spanish-speaking Caribbeans constitute the second-largest Latino group in the United States. Puerto Ricans are the most numerous, closely followed by Cubans and Dominicans. The culinary cultures of Puerto Rico, Cuba, and the Dominican Republic have a common early history, although the development of these cuisines in the United States shows important differences given dissimilar migration conditions. Except for the shared Spanish component, Caribbean Latino cuisines have little in common with Mexican Latino cuisine. Maize and hot chiles, two of the defining ingredients of Mexican cuisine, have only a limited place in Caribbean cooking, which is relatively nonspicy, and is characterized by plantains, yuca (cassava), pork, rice, and beans.

Sixteenth–Nineteenth Centuries

The Arawak Amerindians of the Caribbean are believed to have migrated from South America. The name *Arawak* is related to the indigenous name for yuca, which was their staple food. The Spanish gave the Arawaks of the Caribbean the name *Taínos*. They combined agriculture with fishing, hunting, and gathering. Taíno diet was based on yuca, sweet potato, fish, shellfish, beans, and fruits like papaya, *mamey*, passion fruit, *caimito*, and *cherimoya*. Maize was an important staple even though it arrived only in the fifteenth century.[20]

Taínos like all Arawaks prepared *casabe*, a flat bread made with grated yuca. This bread is still made today in countries like the Dominican Republic and Venezuela, and it is available in specialty markets in the United States. It is simple to make at home using yuca flour but the traditional way to make it is more labor-intensive. Traditionally, yuca is grated, soaked in water, and squeezed several times using an instrument called *sebucán* to remove its toxic components. The pulp is strained to obtain a flour that is cooked on a *budare* (griddle) over a fire. *Casabe* is finally allowed to dry in the sun. The Spanish found the portability of *casabe* very convenient and they always took it with them on their expeditions.

Slavery, war, and new European diseases caused the extermination of Amerindians in the Caribbean roughly 50 years after the arrival of the Spanish, but the culinary influence of Taínos in the Caribbean survived in the food growing and cooking practices that the Spanish and the Africans learned from them. After the disappearance of Taínos, Caribbean cuisine developed in the context of plantation agriculture in which subsistence agriculture plots gave way to large plantations of a single crop for export. The production of sugar, coffee, and tobacco for the global market made the Caribbean dependent on expensive imports for the most basic food needs. Plantation agriculture also implied the forced migration of African slaves. Minimal Amerindian influence, substantial African populations, and dependence on imported foods gave Caribbean culinary culture its distinctive character.

Wheat, olives, and grapes, the key ingredients for Spanish cuisine, did not do well in the Caribbean. Pigs were successfully introduced as they reproduced easily in the wild. The Spanish brought to the islands many ingredients from Mesoamerica like tomatoes, potatoes, cacao, annatto, and vanilla. They also brought from Asia and Africa many ingredients that today seem synonymous with Caribbean food even though they are not indigenous to the region: sugarcane, coffee, coconuts, bananas, mango, and tamarind, among many others. *Bacalao*, a dried and salted codfish from cold northern waters, also became a staple of Caribbean cuisine. This dried fish kept well and it was an important food during the transatlantic voyage. In the plantations, *bacalao* became the cheapest way to feed the slaves. The slaves, who cooked for themselves and for their masters, developed many different ways to cook *bacalao*, which today are considered an important component of the Caribbean culinary repertoire. Boiled and flaked codfish dressed with a little olive oil and served with boiled green bananas, yuca, and underground plant stems like yautía, was food for the slaves and for peasants in Puerto Rico, but today this dish is considered a national dish sporting the romantic name *serenata* (serenade).

Cuba and Puerto Rico did not achieve national independence in the nineteenth century like the rest of Latin America. After losing most of their colonies, Spain encouraged new Spanish immigration to the islands. This and the influx of Spaniards leaving the new independent Latin American countries explains why the cuisine of the islands still has a strong Spanish character. In the nineteenth century the first national cookbooks were published in Cuba and Puerto Rico, and they contain both classic Spanish dishes and *Criollo* specialties that were created in the Caribbean.

In the nineteenth century, New York and Florida were important centers of Puerto Rican and Cuban migration. This early migration included sugar and molasses merchants, tobacco artisan workers, and exiled patriots fighting for the independence of the islands, but the more intense period of Caribbean migration to the United States was in the twentieth century. Because the character of each migration is different in ways that have affected their food culture, each one is discussed separately.

Twentieth Century

Puerto Ricans

In the twentieth century Puerto Rican migration to the United States increased as the political relationship between the two countries became increasingly entangled. Puerto Rico became a possession of the United States at the end of the Spanish-Cuban-American War in 1898. The United States ruled the island first with a military government and then with a civil government headed by an appointed non–Puerto Rican governor. In 1917 all Puerto Ricans acquired a limited U.S. citizenship, which imposed military service but that did not grant the residents of the island the right to vote for the U.S. president, or to have representation with voice and vote in the U.S. Congress. U.S. citizenship did grant the freedom to travel freely between the island and the United States. Puerto Ricans that came to the United States settled mostly in New York City.

Puerto Ricans in New York organized social, cultural, and sports clubs that often sponsored public festivals. The Puerto Rican club *Los jíbaros* (the Puerto Rican peasants) organized festivals that highlighted the preparation of foods like *chicharrones* (fried pork rinds), *tostones* (twice-fried green plantains), and *arroz con dulce* (coconut milk rice pudding).[21] In the late 1920s Puerto Ricans owned more than 125 restaurants and 200 *bodegas* (neighborhood grocery and convenience stores).[22] Puerto Rican migration intensified in the 1950s because of special U.S. government programs intended to attract cheap labor to New York. The mostly rural unskilled migrants settled predominantly in the northeastern part of Manhattan, which is known as *El Barrio* or Spanish Harlem. In *El Barrio* Puerto Ricans strived to continue their food habits. *Carnicerías* (butcher shops), *cuchifritos* (snack stands), and *bodegas* brought Puerto Rican flavors to the neighborhood. In the 1950s Puerto Ricans owned and supported food stalls in the covered food market that they baptized as *La Marqueta*. This market became like a piece of the Caribbean in Manhattan, where they sold yuca and other root vegetables, yautía (underground stem of a plant of the genus Xanthosoma), plantains, green bananas, *culantro* (long leaf cilantro), fruits, *gandules* (pigeon peas), avocados, and *maví* (bark used to make a slightly alcoholic drink).

Bodegas supplemented *La Marqueta* with the convenience of a corner store that also extended credit and cashed checks. *Bodegas* sold dry goods and also served informally as community centers. *La Marqueta* and *bodegas* account for the rise of Goya Foods, an incredibly successful Latino family-run company. In 1928 Prudencio Unanue, a Basque who moved to Puerto Rico when he was 17, opened a small firm in New York to import products like olives, olive

Interior of a *bodega*, New York City, 1950s. The Justo A. Martí Photographic Collection Archives of the Puerto Rican Diaspora, Centro de Estudios Puertorriqueños, Hunter College, CUNY.

oil, and sardines from Spain. In 1936 Unanue founded Goya Foods, which sold rice and beans in bulk in *La Marqueta* and supplied *bodegas* with a wide array of foods for the Puerto Rican table: dried codfish, tropical fruit syrups, papaya and guava preserves, *chorizo* sausages, anchovies, sardines, spices, and cans of prepared foods like *pasteles* (savory plantain and green banana cakes) and *mondongo* (tripe soup).[23] Goya has expanded and diversified according to the changes in migration trends and as the new generations lack the skills to prepare traditional foods. Now Goya is a large food import and processing company that is the leader in its market. In spite of the large size of the company, family members still serve in key positions; they distribute to small stores and employ a largely Spanish-speaking workforce.[24]

Puerto Rican food is not well known outside of Puerto Rican communities but some dishes are served in Cuban, Caribbean, *Criollo*, or "Spanish" restaurants. Puerto Rican restaurants in New York are predominantly *cuchifritos* or snack stands. These snack stands serve Puerto Rican delicacies that are hard to find in other restaurants and that are unlikely to attract the attention of the uninitiated, foods like *morcillas* (blood sausage), pig ears, tongue, and *chicharrones*. They also sell *pasteles*, *bacalaítos* (salted codfish fritters), *rellenos de papa* (meat-stuffed potato croquettes), and tropical fruit drinks.

Cubans

In the 1940s and 1950s there were numerous small Cuban restaurants, butchers, and grocers in New York City.[25] The long-established connection between Cuban and Puerto Rican culinary cultures continued in the New York City context. In the 1960s the character of the Cuban migration changed when hundreds of thousands of Cubans came as refugees. The first wave of Cuban migration after the Cuban Revolution was predominantly composed of landowners, industrialists, managers, and professionals and most of them settled in Miami. The incorporation of Cubans into U.S. society was eased by the Cuban Adjustment Act of 1966, which granted them automatic permanent residence status, unemployment benefits, and free medical care. Their considerable economic and political power distinguishes Cubans from other Latinos. Unlike Mexican, Puerto Rican, and other Latinos, they had enough resources to reproduce the whole range of their food culture from popular food to the most refined.

Between the 1960s and the 1980s Cubans transformed Miami Dade County of Florida into an ever-growing Little Havana. Goya Foods opened a branch in Miami to better serve the Cuban community. Supermarket shelves were lined with Cuban and Latin American brands like *Café Estrella*, *Malta Hatuey*, and *Frijoles Kirby*. Street vendors sold *guarapo* (sugarcane juice), *granizados* (snow cones), *puros* (cigars), pastries, and Cuban coffee. Outside city limits small farmers harvested fruits and vegetables necessary for Cuban cuisine like yuca, *calabaza* (Caribbean pumpkin), *carambola* (star fruit), malanga (underground stem of a plant of the genus Xanthosoma), and *boniato* (sweet potato). *Cantinas* became a successful business of home delivery food services by subscription. They brought hot Cuban meals like roast pork, *boliche* (beef roast stuffed with *chorizo* sausage), and *arroz con pollo* (rice with chicken) every evening to homes throughout the city, allowing women to work and still have traditional family meals at home.[26]

In 1980 a new wave of Cubans came to New York and New Jersey. This new wave of migration was distinguished by its more popular and Afro Cuban background, and by the fact that it did not receive the same kind of benefits as the early one. Cubans from this new wave and from Miami created a vibrant commercial enclave along Bergenline Avenue in Union City, New Jersey. The neighborhood counted with bakeries, butcher shops, grocery stores, nightclubs, and *cantinas* or cafeterias where people could bring their *cantina* aluminum pots to pick up a week's worth of food.[27]

The Cuban restaurant scene is multifaceted. Aside from cafeterias and *cantinas*, there are two other distinctive food establishments: Chinese Cuban restaurants and *Nuevo Cubano* or *Nuevo Latino* restaurants. Chinese Cuban restaurants demonstrate the impact that Chinese migration to Cuba has had on Cuban food habits. These restaurants serve traditional Cuban dishes alongside Chinese dishes prepared the Cuban way. Cuban Chinese fried rice, for example, is distinguished by the generous use of ham. *Nuevo Cubano* or *Nuevo Latino* cuisine is the high-end restaurant interpretation and cross-fertilization of Caribbean and Latin American cuisines in the U.S. context. The higher economic and cultural capital of Cuban Latinos has allowed them to be the pioneers in the creation of the high-end version of the pan-Latino cuisine that is being created by all kinds of Latinos all over the United States.

Dominicans

Dominicans are considered the newest of the Caribbean Latinos in New York. They had been present in the United States before, but their numbers started to increase after the 1961 U.S.-backed military coup against the dictator Rafael Trujillo and the U.S. invasion in 1965. Between 1965 and 1985 Dominicans came from urban middle sectors of the working classes with higher skill levels than their native country's average worker.[28] They settled primarily in New York but also in New Jersey, Florida, Massachusetts, and Rhode Island, among other states. New York City *bodegas* or markets previously owned by Puerto Ricans and Cubans are now predominantly Dominican-owned. Dominicans have also bought small chain supermarkets that were leaving the Latino neighborhoods. Owning a *bodega* is the dream of many immigrants, although the work hours are long and there is the constant threat of being killed by robbers. Dominicans have kept neighborhood grocery stores alive and have enriched Caribbean Latino food culture with dishes like *mangú* (boiled mashed plantains), *chicharrones de pollo* (chicken cracklings), and *chivo guisado* (goat stew). In Washington Heights, where Dominicans constitute the majority of the population, street vendors sell ready-to-eat tropical fruits, *empanadas de yuca* (cassava turnovers), and tropical juices and *batidos* (milk shakes).[29] They also sell bulgur wheat and meat patties called *kipes* or *quipes*. These are the Dominican version of Middle Eastern *kibbeh*, which were brought to the Dominican Republic by Lebanese immigrants.

Puerto Rican, Cuban, and Dominican cuisines have become reacquainted in New York City. The common history added to close proximity in the city accounts for a revitalization of the cuisines and for the creation of a Caribbean Latino cuisine that can be found in homes and restaurants where Cubans, Puerto Ricans, and Dominicans live, cook, and eat together.

CENTRAL AMERICAN CUISINES IN THE UNITED STATES

When the Spanish arrived in Central America, Mayan civilization was extended from contemporary southern México to Guatemala, El Salvador, western Honduras, and Belize. Maya cuisine was based on maize with which they prepared their own varieties of tortillas, tamales, and drinks. Turkey and seafood were high-status foods and the Maya also consumed a wide variety of produce like beans, *jícamas*, sweet potatoes, squashes, avocados, tomatoes, *chayote* squash, pineapples, and papayas. They made sauces with ground roasted squash seeds, chile, annatto, and salt to dress fish or venison.[30] Cacao seeds were so valuable that they were used as currency but chocolate was also drunk with honey, chiles, and sometimes with ground annatto seeds. As elsewhere in Latin America, during the colonial period the Spanish brought new ingredients and Spanish ways of cooking. Rice, wheat, bananas, plantains, pork, chicken, and beef are among the ingredients that were most successfully incorporated. Amerindian and Spanish cuisines were combined over time to create the *cocinas criollas* (creole cuisines) of Central America, the cuisines that are recognized today as national and regional.

Twentieth Century

Central American migration to the United States started as early as 1870 when migrants came to the West Coast with labor and business contracts with coffee and banana companies. Between 1930 and 1970 there were different waves of Central American migration, from men and women of the urban upper and middle classes fleeing dictatorships in Nicaragua and El Salvador in the 1930s to laborers who came to work temporarily or permanently. Central American immigration increased sharply in the late 1970s and 1980s as a result of the political instability in the region.[31] Unlike Cubans, Central Americans were not officially accepted as refugees in the United States and they were not given benefits such as those available under the Cuban Adjustment Act. Most Central American immigrants are largely undocumented and with little education, and they are generally employed in low-paying jobs.[32] These circumstances have made Central Americans less visible and less integrated than other Latinos. Central Americans have settled in Latino neighborhoods predominantly in California, New York, Texas, Florida, Washington, D.C., and Maryland. Salvadorans and Guatemalans constitute the majority of Central Americans in the United States.

The neighborhoods where Salvadorans have settled are recognizable by *pupuserías* where *pupusas*, the most popular Salvadoran food, are served. *Pupusas* are similar to Mexican tortillas because they are disks made with nixtamalized maize *masa*, but they can also be made with rice flour. *Pupusas* are fatter than tortillas and contain a variety of fillings like *chicharrón*, refried beans, cheese flavored with an herb called *loroco*, or a combination of these ingredients in which case they are called *pupusas revueltas*. *Pupusas* are normally served with a pickle or *curtido* of cabbage, carrot, onion, and hot and sweet peppers.

Restaurants in Central American communities serve as gathering places to enjoy a familiar food and atmosphere. Aside from *pupuserías*, most restaurants that serve Salvadoran or any other Central American food are not limited to a single national cuisine and many also serve Mexican food. Since Central Americans are a minority inside the Latino community they adapt the restaurant menus for the larger clientele. Sometimes the Salvadoran or Guatemalan menu is a separate or unwritten menu in a Mexican restaurant available only upon request. Popular Salvadoran menu items are *yuca con chicharrón*, Salvadoran banana leaf–wrapped tamales, and fried ripe plantains with *crema* (cream).

Guatemalan-style fried chicken has become a staple thanks to the successful Guatemalan Pollo Campero fast-food chain. Another popular dish, called the Guatemalan platter, includes meat, fried plantains, rice, and mashed black beans. Honduran menus must include *baleadas*: wheat flour tortillas wrapped around any combination of ingredients like refried beans, avocado, shredded cheese, *crema*, eggs, jalapeño peppers, simmered beef, and onion. Nicaraguan specialties offered in restaurants in the United States include *gallo pinto* (rice and red beans cooked with onions and peppers), and *nacatamales*, Nicaraguan tamales that are also popular in El Salvador and Honduras. Panamanian and Costa Rican food is almost unknown in the United States due to the small number of immigrants from these countries. In general, the availability of Central American food in restaurants is limited to a few representative dishes, although a wide range of ingredients is generally available for people to cook at home. Goya Foods and other food importers and distributors constantly expand their line of products to satisfy the demand for Central American ingredients.

SOUTH AMERICAN CUISINES IN THE UNITED STATES

South American cultures and cuisines are different from Mexican, Caribbean, and Central American ones in significant ways. Before the arrival of the Spanish, the Inca empire stretched along the Andes mountain region including large areas of contemporary Ecuador, Bolivia, Perú, Argentina, and Chile. The Inca empire was one of the largest and most sophisticated civilizations of the Americas. It comprised many different ethnic groups and their dominant languages were Quechua and Aymara. Andean Amerindian cultures are very different from the Maya and the Aztec, and the differences are evident in their cuisine as well. Aside from maize, potatoes were the most important staple for the Inca. Potatoes are native to the Perú region and the International Potato Center lists 3,800 traditional Andean cultivated varieties. Among the many unique Andean ways of preparing potatoes, the freeze-dried *chuño* stands out. To make *chuño* the Inca exposed small potatoes to the extreme cold during a few nights and during the day they pressed them with their feet and exposed them to the sun to remove all moisture. The result is a product that keeps for years and that is used to prepare a wide variety of sweet and savory dishes. The Inca also consumed the highly nutritious grain called *quinoa*, many kinds of tubers, seafood, llama meat, and dried meat and fish. Perú became the center of another important Viceroyalty during the Spanish colonial period, which allowed the region to conserve some distinctiveness. The Andean culinary culture present in regions of Bolivia, Chile, Colombia, Ecuador, Perú, and Venezuela is one of the most distinctive in South America.

Other regions of South America have their own culinary character. The cuisine of Paraguay and parts of Brazil and Argentina has been shaped by the culture of indigenous peoples like the Guaraní who use yuca as a staple with which they make a full range of dishes. South American countries like Venezuela, Colombia, and Brazil have Caribbean regions in which the culinary culture is similar to the rest of the Caribbean, and countries like Perú have significant Chinese and Japanese elements in their culinary culture. While Brazilian cuisine has much in common with the rest of South America, it also has a distinctive cuisine of its own because of its large territory, because of its Portuguese rather than Spanish colonial heritage, and because of its own mix of Amerindian, European, African, and Asian populations.

The cuisine of Argentina, Chile, and Uruguay has a stronger European character than other Latin American countries. The Amerindians that inhabited this region were nomadic or seminomadic small groups and many of them did not survive colonization. The base of the cuisine of the region is Amerindian staples like corn, Spanish cooking, and the abundance of beef since the cattle introduced by the Spanish found optimum conditions for their propagation. In the nineteenth century millions of European immigrants settled in Argentina, Chile, Uruguay, Perú, and Venezuela. Most of them came from Italy but there were also significant numbers of German, French, English, and Slavic immigrants. All these groups have left their mark in contemporary South American culinary culture. Only in the late twentieth century have South American countries become countries that send rather than receive immigrants.

South Americans in the United States are the smallest Latino group and, like Central Americans, they are mostly foreign-born and have immigrated in large numbers only since the 1980s. Colombians, who have come seeking refuge from political violence, are the largest subgroup. Ecuadorians and Peruvians are the second-largest group followed by much smaller numbers of Argentineans, Bolivians, Brazilians, Chileans, Paraguayans, Uruguayans, and Venezuelans. Many South American Latinos are middle class and well educated but have typically experienced downward economic and social mobility as a result of migration to the United States.[33] A famous example is María Piedad Cano, known as the "*Arepa* Lady." Cano was a judge in Medellín, Colombia, and she came to the United States to escape political violence. She had never before made *arepas* but now her *arepa* pushcart in Queens, New York, is a food lover's destination.[34] For immigrants, selling food from their native countries is a common way of supplementing insufficient incomes, and sometimes it is the first step toward successful entrepreneurship.

The main destination for Colombians from the Caribbean coast is Florida, whereas for those from the inland it is New York. Colombian cuisine varies significantly by region since the country contains territory in the Caribbean coast, the Andean mountains, and the plains area, and the main cities of Bogotá, Cali, and Medellín have also developed their own specialty dishes. In Queens, a New York City borough with a large Colombian population, one can find Colombian specialties from different regions, often in the same establishments. Queens boasts many Colombian restaurants that also feature live music and sometimes organize cultural and literary events. They serve Colombian breakfasts throughout the morning and late dinners from 10:00 P.M. to 11:00 P.M. Street foods sold from carts and trucks are very popular, as are the bakeries that sell Colombian baked goods like *pandebono* (cheese and yuca bread rolls) and snacks like sausage with *arepas* and empanadas (turnovers).

Ecuadorians have settled predominantly in New York and they have a strong presence in Queens. They have made *ceviche* (citrus-marinated raw seafood) widely available both on the streets and in pan-Latino restaurants. Ecuadorian restaurants often feature a dish called *caldo de bola*, which is a ball made with plantain that is stuffed with beef and vegetables and served in a meat and vegetable soup. Roasted *cuy* (guinea pig) is an Ecuadorian delicacy that is available by special order in some restaurants and frozen *cuy* to cook at home can be found in some Latino supermarkets.

The largest wave of Peruvian immigrants came in the 1980s and they live in Chicago, Miami, and Los Angeles and in the suburbs of New Jersey and New York. Many of them came as college students or to work as technicians. Peruvian cuisine is well known for its *ceviches* and for seafood dishes like *chupe de camarones* (shrimp chowder) and *sopa de mariscos* (seafood soup). Peruvians make use of many varieties of chiles, corn, and potatoes that are unique to the Andean region. Marinated rotisserie chickens are the best-known specialty sold in neighborhoods where Peruvians have settled, but restaurants serving a full Peruvian menu can also be found. Peruvian food is increasingly available outside of Latino neighborhoods because of medium-scale restaurants that cater to a wide clientele. Even though the number of Peruvians is relatively small, Peruvian food is so distinctive that it is making a clear mark on pan-Latino cuisine.

Argentinean immigrants came predominantly from medium and higher economic sectors mostly during the 1970s and 1980s, while Brazilians are generally from a middle-class background and have come mostly in the past 20 years. Although their numbers are relatively small, the Argentinean, Brazilian, and Uruguayan tradition of barbecuing sausages and many different cuts of beef in steakhouses called *parrillas* by Argentineans and *churrascarias* by Brazilians has become widespread in the United States. Brazilians and Argentineans have been able to open medium and upscale restaurants that popularize their cuisine outside of ethnic enclaves. The food of Latinos from other South American countries exists almost exclusively at home, although restaurants of all Latino nationalities can be found.

NOTES

1. Bernardino de Sahagún, *General History of the Things of New Spain*, Book 10: "The People" (Santa Fe, N.M.: School of American Research, 1953–82), p. 69.

2. Bernardino de Sahagún, *General History of the Things of New Spain*, Book 8: "Kings and Lords" (Santa Fe, N.M.: School of American Research, 1953–82), pp. 37–40.

3. Jeffrey M. Pilcher, "Tex-Mex, Cal-Mex, New Mex, or Whose Mex? Notes on the Historical Geography of Southwestern Cuisine," *Journal of the Southwest* 43, no. 4 (Winter 2001): 659–680.

4. Janet Long-Solís and Luis Alberto Vargas, *Food Culture in Mexico* (Westport, Conn.: Greenwood Press, 2005), pp. 98–121.

5. Arthur L. Campa, *Hispanic Culture in the Southwest* (Norman: University of Oklahoma Press, 1979), p. 280.

6. Rosaura Sánchez, *Telling Identities: The Californio Testimonios* (Berkeley: University of California Press, 1995), p. 75.

7. Sánchez, *Telling Identities*, pp. 52, 58.

8. Campa, *Hispanic Culture in the Southwest*, pp. 277–281.

9. Mario Montaño, "Appropriation and Counterhegemony in South Texas: Food Slurs, Offal Meats, and Blood," in *Usable Pasts: Traditions and Group Expressions in North America*, ed. Tad Tuleja (Logan: Utah State University Press, 1997), p. 51.

10. Donna R. Gabaccia, *We Are What We Eat: Ethnic Food and the Making of Americans* (Cambridge, Mass.: Harvard University Press, 1998), p. 128.

11. Víctor Valle, "A Curse of Tea and Potatoes: The Life and Recipes of Encarnación Pinedo," in *Encarnación's Kitchen: Mexican Recipes from Nineteenth-Century California*, ed. and trans. Dan Strehl (Berkeley: University of California Press, 2003), pp. 6–7.

12. Valle, "Curse of Tea and Potatoes," p. 5.

13. Dan Strehl, ed., trans., *Encarnación's Kitchen: Mexican Recipes from Nineteenth-Century California* (Berkeley: University of California Press, 2003), pp. 47–49.

14. Víctor M. Valle, *Recipe of Memory: Five Generations of Mexican Cuisine* (New York: New Press, 1995), pp. 107–115.

15. Daniel D. Arreola, *Tejano South Texas: A Mexican American Cultural Province* (Austin: University of Texas Press, 2002), pp. 163–164.

16. Robb Walsh, *Tex-Mex: A History in Recipes and Photos* (New York: Broadway Books, 2004), pp. 68–69.

17. Amy Bentley, "From Culinary Other to Mainstream America: Meanings and Uses of Southwestern Cuisine," in *Culinary Tourism*, ed. Lucy M. Long (Lexington: University Press of Kentucky, 2004), p. 211.

18. Víctor M. Valle and Rodolfo D. Torres, *Latino Metropolis* (Minneapolis: University of Minnesota Press, 2000), pp. 67–100.

19. Cindy Price, "Chasing the Perfect Taco up the California Coast," *New York Times*, July 21, 2006.

20. José Rafael Lovera, *Gastronomía caribeña: Historia, recetas y bibliografía* (Caracas: CEGA, 1991), pp. 27–31.

21. Jorge Duany, *The Puerto Rican Nation on the Move: Identities on the Island and in the United States* (Chapel Hill: University of North Carolina Press, 2002), p. 188.

22. Duany, *Puerto Rican Nation on the Move*, p. 198.

23. Joel Denker, *The World on a Plate: A Tour through the History of America's Ethnic Cuisines* (Boulder, Colo.: Westview Press, 2003), pp. 149–152.

24. Gabaccia, *We Are What We Eat*, p. 166.

25. Lisa Maya Knauer, "Eating in Cuban," in *Mambo Montage: The Latinization of New York*, ed. Agustín Laó-Montes and Arlene Dávila (New York: Columbia University Press, 2001), p. 431.

26. María Cristina García, *Havana USA: Cuban Exiles and Cuban-Americans in South Florida, 1959–1994* (Berkeley: University of California Press, 1996), pp. 87–88.

27. Denker, *World on a Plate*, p. 155.

28. Ramón Grosfoguel, "Latino Caribbean Diasporas in New York," in *Mambo Montage*, ed. Laó-Montes and Dávila, p. 98.

29. Inés M. Miyares, "Changing Latinization of New York City," in *Hispanic Spaces, Latino Places: Community and Cultural Diversity in Contemporary America*, ed. Daniel D. Arreola (Austin: University of Texas Press, 2004), p. 160.

30. Sophie D. Coe, *America's First Cuisines* (Austin: University of Texas Press, 1994), p. 164.

31. Carlos B. Cordova, *The Salvadoran Americans* (Westport, Conn.: Greenwood Press, 2005), pp. 55–68.

32. Daniel D. Arreola, "Hispanic American Legacy, Latino American Diaspora," in *Hispanic Spaces, Latino Places*, ed. Arreola, p. 20.

33. Arreola, "Hispanic American Legacy, Latino American Diaspora," p. 20.

34. Dana Bowen, "Street Corner Cooks Have Names, Too," *New York Times*, September 22, 2004.

2

Major Foods and Ingredients

Latino cuisines are based on a common set of ingredients like maize, beans, rice, squash, plantains, yuca, and chiles. This does not mean that Latino cuisines are homogenous or repetitive. The ingredients are processed, combined, and prepared in so many different ways that the possibilities seem endless. Each Latino cuisine emphasizes a different selection of the shared ingredients, seasonings, and techniques, creating clearly differentiated culinary traditions. In the United States many Latin American ingredients are unavailable. The lack of local herbs and vegetables, and of the specific varieties of common ingredients like maize and potatoes, is blurring the distinctiveness of different Latino cuisines since they all depend on the same reduced pool of ingredients. However, new ingredients have also been incorporated and they are given new uses according to Latino culinary logic.

GRAINS

Maize

Maize (*Zea mays*) is the staple that gives Latino cuisine a cohesive identity. In the United States, as in many Latin American cities, cooking with maize often does not mean starting with a fresh or dried ear of maize but the use of a variety of maize flours and products. Home processing of maize is laborious and time-consuming, which is incompatible with busy work schedules. The United States is the largest producer of maize in the world but only a small fraction of the harvest is consumed as corn and cornmeal. The greatest part of the maize grown in the United States is of a variety called field corn, which cannot be eaten without processing. Field corn is used to feed livestock, to make products like corn syrup, corn starch, and corn oil, and to produce ethanol and other nonfood products. Mesoamerican and Andean peoples are used to consuming and appreciating many different varieties of maize but delicacies that depend on specific varieties of maize are uncommon in the U.S. Latino food culture. The corn that is available at supermarkets does not have enough starch to make the basic *masa* (dough) for Mexican and Central American foods like tortillas, *pupusas* (Salvadoran stuffed tortillas), and tamales. Mexican and Central American *masa* is a dough made with nixtamalized maize, which is dried maize that has been boiled and soaked in a slaked lime solution. The preferred maize to make *masa* is called *cacahuazintle* and it is available in Mexican markets. Dent corn is a good alternative but it is not as easy to find since it is not being produced for human consumption. Fresh *masa* is rarely made at home but it is increasingly available in Mexican stores and *tortillerías* (tortilla shops). For daily home use, Mexican and Central American Latinos buy ready-made tortillas or use a dried and powdered nixtamalized maize dough known as *masa harina* after a popular brand name. This flour is different from the cornmeal that is generally available in supermarkets because the nixtamalization treatment changes the flavor and texture. A different maize product used by South American Latinos is a precooked (but not nixtamalized) maize flour called *arepa* flour, used both for *arepas* (maize griddle cakes) and for some South American tamales. Whereas foods prepared with these products do not have the same flavor and aroma of those made with freshly processed maize, both *masa harina* and *arepa* flour significantly simplify the preparation of well-loved dishes, allowing them to remain a part of Latino food culture. Maize can be served in one way or another for breakfast, lunch, and dinner. There are appetizers, main dishes, accompaniments, desserts, alcoholic and nonalcoholic drinks that feature maize as their main ingredient.

Nixtamalized *masa* is used principally by Mexican Americans and Central Americans in the United States to make the maize tortillas that are a part of daily meals. It is also used to make many Mexican *antojitos* (snacks) like *chalupas* (deep-fried boat-shaped *masa* filled with meat and salsa), gorditas (small fat tortillas with a variety of fillings), and *sopes* (flat baskets of *masa* with savory fillings and garnishes on top), as well as to make the Salvadoran *pupusas*. After tortillas, the most important use of nixtamalized *masa* is to make tamales. Mexican tamales come in many varieties but most of them use nixtamalized *masa* and are wrapped in corn husks before steaming. Some tamales, like *tamales de elote* and *corundas*, are made with fresh maize while others, like *tamales costeños*, are wrapped in banana leaves. The nixtamalized *masa* is traditionally prepared with lard but, because of health concerns and because the lard available in the United States is considered flavorless, it is often substituted or combined with other fats like butter or vegetable shortening. The *masa* can be filled with a savory or a sweet filling but the latter is less frequent in the United States. The most common traditional fillings for Mexican tamales are pork, chicken, or beef mixed with red or green salsa or with *mole poblano* (sauce made with dried chiles, nuts, and chocolate). Latinos and non-Latinos alike have experimented widely with tamales and it is not strange to find vegetarian tamales and tamales filled with all kinds of ingredients. Natural wrappers—fresh or dried corn husks and banana leaves—are sometimes substituted or combined with aluminum foil, which is more convenient but does not contribute to the aroma of the tamales. Another difference in the way that tamales are prepared by Latinos in the United States is that they are often served on a plate with a sauce instead of plain as finger food as in México.

Salvadoran Americans and other Central Americans make their own varieties of maize tamales, including *tamales de elote* made with fresh maize, and tamales made with nixtamalized *masa* and a wide range of fillings. They often cook the *masa* in chicken stock before assembling the tamales, which gives them a softer texture and more complex flavor. The use of banana leaves instead of corn husks to wrap the tamales also gives them a different aroma. A common Salvadoran filling is cooked pork or chicken and a few olives and capers. Guatemalan tamales have varieties called *paches* or *chuchitos*. Some of them contain additional ingredients in the *masa*, like tomato sauce, mashed potato, annatto, and allspice, and they might contain a single large piece of cooked meat as filling. Nicaraguan tamales, called *nacatamales*, are larger and contain many more ingredients than most tamales. The *masa* for *nacatamales* contains ingredients like milk, mashed potato, onion, garlic, and bell pepper. The filling is chicken or pork with a fresh tomato and vinegar sauce, and there is also a substantial topping of rice, olives, raisins, sliced tomato, sliced potato, and a prune.

South American Latinos also make maize tamales and other related maize treats that have their own distinct names. Colombian tamales vary by region but they generally use precooked maize flour (not nixtamalized) for the *masa* and banana leaves as wrappers. Popular filling combinations are pork rind with tomato, hard-boiled egg with chicken or pork, and pork and chicken with *longaniza* sausage. Venezuelan tamales are called *hallacas* and they are also made with precooked maize flour and wrapped in banana leaves. The *masa* is flavored and colored with annatto and the filling contains stewed chicken, pork, and beef with a garnish of almonds, raisins, roasted red pepper strips, olives, and pickled vegetables. While *hallacas* are considered special fare made only for Christmas or special occasions, a simpler and more common category of tamales made by Venezuelans, Colombians, and Ecuadorians is *bollos*. These can be made with fresh maize or with precooked maize *masa* and they can be plain or have a filling made with leftovers.

Humitas are the beloved fresh maize tamales of South America. The sweet corn available in the United States has too much moisture to make *humitas* that hold their shape, but this is usually solved by adding cornmeal or *masa harina*, or by using imported frozen maize. Ecuadorian *humitas* mix ground fresh maize with cheese, eggs, and butter or lard, and a chile condiment called *ají criollo*. Colombian *humitas* contain ground pork rind, and Peruvian ones are flavored with cilantro, garlic, and chiles. Argentinean *humitas* are seasoned with onion and tomato and there are numerous additional variations.

Arepas are another maize treat associated mostly with Colombians and Venezuelans, although they are made by other South American Latinos as well. Venezuelan *arepas*, particularly the stuffed variety, are growing in popularity in the United States among Latinos and non-Latinos alike. They are round flat sweet or savory cakes made with precooked white or yellow maize flour and cooked on a griddle. Thicker varieties are finished in the oven to make sure that the interior is fully cooked. The arepa is split open and the interior is simply filled with butter or cheese, or with more elaborate filling combinations like beans and cheese (called *arepa de dominó*), avocado, chicken, potatoes, carrots, and mayonnaise (called *reina pepiada*), and cheese and shredded beef (called *arepa pelúa*), among many others. Colombian *arepas* are thinner and are eaten with cheese or butter on top, while *arepas de queso* already contain cheese in the dough. Cooked Colombian *arepas* are sold in Latino neighborhoods to be frozen and reheated in a toaster oven, which has made it possible to enjoy them for breakfast or as a snack more frequently. A variety of plain and bland *arepas* is used as a simple breakfast with a cup of chocolate or to accompany flavorful meals like stews and *chorizo* sausage. There are also sweet *arepas* and fresh maize *arepas*. In New York and Miami street fairs an *arepa* mozzarella cheese sandwich, grilled cheese style, has become very popular.

Maize has a less important role in the cuisine of Caribbean Latinos but it is still used to make cheese and cornmeal fritters like the *sorullitos* made by Puerto Ricans. Caribbean cuisines have their own version of maize tamales, called *guanimes de maíz*. Puerto Rican *guanimes* are made with plain cornmeal (neither precooked nor nixtamalized), coconut milk, and molasses. They are wrapped in banana leaves, boiled, and served to accompany savory dishes like stewed salted codfish. Dominican *guanimes de maíz* are savory appetizers made with plain cornmeal and filled with seasoned ground meat. Cubans make fresh maize tamales that traditionally have a pork filling. Dessert and breakfast dishes made of cornmeal mush, sometimes flavored with coconut milk, were popular at one time among Caribbean Latinos but have now given way to other desserts and to industrial breakfast products like corn flakes.

Latinos enjoy maize in many other ways. Maize flour is used to make the dough for some empanadas (turnovers). Mexican *atoles* (nixtamalized maize *masa* drinks) can be easily made with *masa harina* or with flavored instant mixes. Maize—fresh, nixtamalized, or as *masa*—is added to a variety of soups and stews. Fresh maize is also enjoyed boiled, steamed, grilled, or baked as a side dish.

Humitas (South American Fresh Maize Tamales)

6 ears of sweet corn, husks
  on (4 cups kernels)
1 TBSP basil leaves,
  roughly chopped
1 small jalapeño or serrano
  chile, finely minced

1/4 cup fine cornmeal
4 TBSP butter or lard
1 onion, chopped
1 garlic clove, minced
1/2 TBSP salt

Peel the ears of corn without tearing the leaves. Reserve the more pliable inner leaves for wrapping the *humitas* and tear some of the broken ones to form long strips to tie them. Rinse the corn and remove the silk. Use a knife to cut the kernels from the cobs and use the blunt side to scrape the milk out. Puree the maize kernels in a food processor or blender with the basil, chile, and cornmeal to form a thick paste. Heat the butter or lard in a pot or large skillet over medium heat and sauté the onions and garlic for 3 minutes, or until soft. Add the maize puree and salt, and cook stirring constantly for 10–15 minutes or until the mixture thickens and separates from the bottom of the pot or skillet. It should have the consistency of mashed potatoes.

To assemble the humitas, place ⅓ cup filling on the broader bottom half of a corn husk. Fold the edges over the filling, starting on the sides, to form a square package of approximately 3–3 1/2 inches by 1 1/2–2 inches. Tie the *humitas* using strips of husk or kitchen twine. Steam the *humitas* lying flat in the steamer for 40 minutes. Let them cool and firm slightly before serving. Serve in the opened husks with a hot sauce like *ají criollo* or with an onion and tomato salad on the side.

Rice

Rice is the daily staple for Caribbean Latinos, including those whose origins are traced back to the Caribbean coasts of Central and South America. Both medium and long grain rice varieties are used according to personal preference. The wide variety of ways to prepare rice is classified according to the color or the appearance of the rice, and according to the main ingredient combinations. The most common rice preparations are white rice and yellow or red rice. Many people like to cook rice slowly in a heavy bottomed pot until the bottom layer gets crispy. This crispy layer, called *pegao* by Puerto Ricans and *concón* by Dominicans, is scraped out and enjoyed as a delicacy. White rice can be cooked plainly with water and salt or seasoned with sautéed onions and garlic and cooked in chicken stock. Yellow or red rice is seasoned like white rice and colored with tomatoes and annatto. Mexicans have a specialty green rice that gets its color from poblano peppers and parsley. Peruvians prepare their own version of Spanish black rice that gets its dramatic color from squid ink. Colombian black rice, on the other hand, is cooked with coconut and gets the black color from raisins and molasses.

Rice and beans is a classic combination. Each Latino group has a favorite bean for it and some even have distinctive whimsical names. Cubans serve white rice with black beans that they call *moros y cristianos*, which literally means "Moors and Christians." Another Cuban rice and bean combination is *arroz congrí*, which is made with red beans. Both Costa Ricans and Nicaraguans call their rice and beans *gallo pinto* (spotted rooster) but Costa Ricans favor black beans while Nicaraguans prefer red beans. These names refer to the visual appeal of the dish whereas other names refer to the idea of rice and beans as a wedding as in the Salvadorian *casamiento*. A whimsical name for a mashed beans and rice patty is *tacu-tacu*, a regional dish of Perú.

While *paella* is a regional specialty of Spain reserved for festive occasions, simpler rice and meat and/or seafood combinations are enjoyed by Latinos more frequently. The most common one is *arroz con pollo*, which is a red/yellow rice cooked with chicken. Other popular combinations are rice with shrimp and rice with sausage. Dominican rice, meat, and vegetable combinations are called *locrio*, while rice, beans, and vegetable combinations are known as *arroz moro*. A Puerto Rican rice specialty is *asopao*, a soupy rice with meat or seafood. Chinese fried rice is another combination dish that has been part of Latino cuisine for a long time.

Latinos in general use rice to make rice and milk desserts known as *arroz con leche*. Puerto Ricans also make *arroz con dulce*, which is a rice and coconut milk porridge that is flavored with cinnamon and thick enough to cut with a knife.

Wheat

Wheat is consumed by Latinos in the form of bread, pasta, tortillas, turnovers, and sweets. While maize breads like tortillas and *arepas* and yuca breads like *casabe* and *pandebono* are important, wheat breads also have a significant role in Latino cuisine. Neighborhood *panaderías* provide the regional bread specialties that Latinos buy rather than make at home. Caribbean Latinos look for *pan criollo*, a soft-crusted French-style loaf that is eaten with butter or is used to make sandwiches like the famous *sandwich cubano*. They also value a yellow-colored elongated soft bun that is indispensable for lighter sandwiches called *media luna* (half moon). Mexican *panaderías* offer *bolillos*, the oval-shaped hard-crusted rolls necessary to make Mexican-style sandwiches called *tortas*. Sweet bread rolls in different shapes are very popular for breakfasts and snacks, and there are also fancier breads for special occasions like *pan de muerto* for the Day of the Dead, and *rosca de reyes* for Three Kings Day.

Turnovers are a beloved treat for all Latinos although they vary enormously. Empanadas receive different names like *empanaditas*, *pasteles*, *pastelitos*, and *pastelillos*. They can be large like a pie or small like an appetizer, baked or fried, sweet or savory. Certain fillings have become classics but empanadas are versatile and can be filled with leftovers or with fancy ingredient combinations. The most popular fillings are ground meat, cheese, or guava but there are also more elaborate versions that contain stewed meats and vegetables.

Wheat flour is used to make a wide range of fritters, transformed from a common Spanish origin. *Buñuelos* is a generic name for fritters that includes Mexican flat fritters served with cinnamon and sugar, Colombian round white cheese fritters, and Caribbean egg-rich round fritters served in syrup. *Churros* are long fritters made with wheat flour, eggs, and milk that are rolled in sugar after frying. A fritter popularized by Mexicans in the Southwest is *sopaipillas*. These are thin geometrical shapes made with plain wheat flour dough that puff up when fried and that can be served with honey and cinnamon or with savory accompaniments. A similar thin fried cracker favored by Dominicans is a version of the Johnny cake called *yaniqueques*.

The favorite wheat flour–based Latino dessert is *pastel tres leches* (three milk cake). This is a light cake that is soaked in a combination of fresh milk or cream, evaporated milk, and condensed milk, and finished with a layer of meringue or whipped cream. Birthday and special celebration layered cakes with fanciful decorations are also popular. Another dessert widely enjoyed by Latinos is *alfajores*. These are sweet biscuit sandwiches filled with dulce de leche and covered with chocolate, powdered sugar, or coconut. Puff pastry treats, filled with guava paste or with sweetened cream cheese, are a favorite of Cuban Americans and Puerto Ricans.

Pasta in all its varieties is more frequently enjoyed by South Americans than by other Latinos for whom pasta has a rather limited role. Pasta and pizza are a fundamental part of Argentinean and Uruguayan culinary culture. The most common pasta used by other Latinos is thin noodles for soups and tube shapes for quick and inexpensive salads and casseroles.

ROOTS, TUBERS, AND OTHER STARCHY STAPLES

Bananas and Plantains

Green bananas are used as a vegetable in Latino cuisine. They can be plainly boiled and served as a side dish, or added to thick stews called *sancochos*. Grated green bananas are an ingredient of the dough used by Puerto Ricans to make *pasteles* (root vegetable tamales) and *alcapurrias* (yautía and green banana fritters stuffed with seasoned ground meat). Puerto Ricans and Dominicans also prepare them as *guineítos en escabeche*, lightly pickled in vinegar, olive oil, onion, and garlic.

Plantains look like bananas but they are larger and have to be cooked to be enjoyed green or ripe. There are plantain recipes for each level of ripeness, from totally green to half ripe and fully ripe. Green plantains are starchier and they are the best choice to make razor-thin chips called *chifles* and *mariquitas*. *Tostones*, *patacones*, or *tachinos* are different names for thicker twice-fried green plantain slices. *Mangú*, a dish used as a marker of Dominican identity, is made with mashed boiled unripe plantains mixed with oil, vinegar, and onion. Puerto Ricans prefer *mofongo*, a similar dish made with fried green plantains pounded with garlic and *chicharrón* (pork rinds). Another Puerto Rican preparation is fried clusters of long green plantain shreds that are called *arañitas* (little spiders). Grated or boiled green plantain is used to make plain or stuffed balls that are added to stews. Unripe plantains are also used to make tamales and to make dough for turnovers. Together with yuca and other tubers, green plantains are an important component of the thick meat and tuber stews called *sancochos* that are a fundamental part of many Latino cuisines. Frozen packages containing cut and peeled green plantains and tubers are used for quick *sancochos*.

Ripe plantains are fried and served as an accompaniment to any meal. In this case they receive the name *maduros* or *tajadas*. Caribbean Latinos layer long slices of ripe plantain with meat or chicken to make *pastelones*. Sometimes whole ripe plantains are caramelized and served as dessert. The skin of the plantain turns black when it is at its sweetest.

Tostones (Twice-Fried Plantains)

2 large green plantains	Salt
Oil for deep frying	

Trim the ends of the plantains. Make three lengthwise incisions on the skins of the plantains and use the edge of the knife to peel them. Cut the plantains into 1-inch diagonal slices. Heat 2 inches of oil in a heavy-bottomed pot over medium heat and fry the slices until soft. Work in batches as necessary to avoid crowding the pot. Remove the plantains with a slotted spoon and drain on absorbent paper. Flatten the plantains to half their thickness using your fist, two flat plates, or a specially designed *tostonera* press. Raise the heat to medium high and fry the plantains again until crisp and golden. Drain on absorbent paper, season with salt to taste, and serve warm.

Jícama

Jícamas are turnip-shaped roots with a light brown skin and white flesh. They can be eaten raw and have a refreshing crispy texture. Jícamas are favored by Mexicans more than by other Latinos. They are used in salads, salsas, and pickled.

Potatoes

Potatoes originated in the Andean region and currently the Peruvian-based International Potato Center recognizes no fewer than 3,800 traditional Andean cultivated potatoes. South American cuisines exploit the specific qualities of different kinds of potatoes, although in the United States the range of potatoes available is limited to a handful of varieties. Peruvian *papa amarilla* (yellow potato) is a highly flavorful floury potato used to make *causas*. This dish consists of spicy mashed potato cakes layered with savory fillings. In the United States Yukon Gold potatoes are sometimes used for this dish but

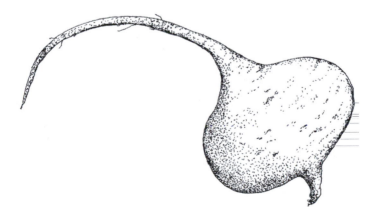

Jícama. © J. Susan Cole Stone.

people prefer to use the tastier *papa amarilla*, which is available frozen. *Papas a la huancaína* is a Peruvian specialty of potatoes dressed with a sauce made of the mild chile *ají amarillo*. Ecuadorians make *llapingachos*, which are potato and cheese patties that can make a meal when served with eggs or sausage and a salad. Peruvians and Ecuadorians use freeze dried potatoes (*chuño*) to make specialty dishes. The Colombian potato variety called *papa criolla* is indispensable for Colombian chicken stew. Latinos in general add potatoes to soups, stews, empanadas, and tamales, and also enjoy them French fried as a side dish. Potato croquettes like the Puerto Rican meat-filled *rellenos de papa* are also common.

Sweet Potatoes

Called *boniato, batata,* and *camote,* the Latin American sweet potato is less sweet than the ones widely available in the United States. They have red skin and white flesh and they are boiled or fried. Sweet potatoes are a classic accompaniment to lime-marinated *ceviches* because they balance the acidity. Mashed and stuffed sweet potato dishes are other ways in which sweet potatoes are used in Latino cuisine.

Yams

Ñames are large white or pale yellow tubers not to be confused with sweet potatoes, which are called yams in the United States. Like other tubers, *ñames* are boiled, mashed, or added to stews like *sancocho*.

Boniato. © J. Susan Cole Stone.

Yautía and Malanga

Yautía and malanga are underground stems of a plant of the genus Xanthosoma that is indigenous to the Caribbean. They have a brown and hairy exterior and are long with one round and one tapered end. There are different species including those with yellow, white, and purple flesh. There is a misconception that malanga and yautía are different Cuban and Puerto Rican names for the same food, but for Latino cuisine connoisseurs malanga and yellow, purple, and white yautías are four related but distinct corms and they are valued according to differences in taste and flouriness. White yautía is the most easily available and it is eaten boiled, in stews, or mashed. Grated yautía is an indispensable ingredient in the dough used for Puerto Rican *pasteles* (green banana savory cakes) and *alcapurrias* (meat-stuffed fritters).

Yuca

Yuca, cassava, or manioc is a long root with tapered ends that has a thick brown skin, a thin pink intermediate layer, and snowy white flesh. Yuca was the main staple for Caribbean Amerindians and it still has that role in the diet of the indigenous peoples of the Amazon region. In Caribbean and South American cuisines yuca has as many uses as any other staple. There is sweet yuca and bitter yuca that needs to be processed to remove poisonous cyanogenic glucosides. Sweet yuca is the kind that is sold fresh or frozen in supermarkets in the United States. Fresh sweet yuca is highly perishable even when it is coated with a wax layer to preserve freshness. This explains the popularity of frozen yuca, which is of better quality and ready to cook. Bitter

Yuca. © J. Susan Cole Stone.

yuca is processed to make different kinds of yuca flours and starches. Brazilians toast yuca flour (also called manioc meal) to make *farofa*, a condiment that is sprinkled on savory dishes. Yuca starch—sold as tapioca starch, *almidón de yuca*, and *yuca harina*—is used to make breads, pastries, and cakes.

Boiled sweet yuca is eaten as a side dish plain or *al ajillo*, dressed with olive oil and garlic. It is added to thick stews and it is used to make dough for tamales and empanadas. Ground or mashed yuca is also used to make many different kinds of plain and stuffed fritters. One of the most popular fritters is the Panamanian *carimañola* that has a ground meat filling. Another popular fritter is *buñuelos de yuca*, of which there are both sweet and cheese versions, and Dominicans make savory yuca turnovers called *cativías*.

Bitter yuca is used to make the crisp flat bread *casabe* that is an important meal accompaniment in traditional Venezuelan and Dominican meals. In the United States Latinos buy *casabe* in specialty markets rather than make it at home because bitter yuca is not available and its processing requires a fair amount of time and skill. Yuca breads made with yuca starch are made at home or bought in *panaderías*. Colombian bakeries sell yuca and cheese bread rolls called *pandebonos*, as well as other yuca breads and sweets. The white flower of the yuca plant, called *flor de izote*, is a delicacy highly esteemed in Salvadoran cooking.

Yuca con mojo (Cuban Yuca in Citrus-Garlic Sauce)

1 1/2 pound frozen yuca	1/2 tsp dried oregano
5 minced garlic cloves	1/4 tsp cumin
Juice of 1 lime	Salt and pepper to taste
1/2 cup olive oil	

Steam the yuca for 30 minutes and allow it to cool. Remove the stringy fibers from the core and cut the flesh into bite-sized pieces. Toss the yuca pieces with the rest of the ingredients and cook in a sauté pan over medium heat for 5 minutes or until lightly browned.

BEANS

Beans are a mainstay of Latino cuisines. They are a nutritious side dish and they also appear in soups, stews, and salads. There are many different varieties of beans and each Latino cuisine has a favored kind for specific dishes. Pinto is the favorite bean for Mexican refried beans, while Salvadorans prefer red beans. Red or pinto beans are used by Hondurans in their *baleadas*, which are similar to bean burritos. Red beans are used by Dominicans to make the bean dessert *habichuelas con dulce*. Black beans are the classic choice for many Cuban dishes like *moros y cristianos*, and for the hearty Brazilian bean stew *feijoada completa*. South Americans prefer navy, fava, lupini, and Lima beans to make salads. For festive occasions, Puerto Ricans and Panamanian Americans look for *gandules* (pigeon peas) to pair with rice. *Garbanzos* (chickpeas) are widely used in dishes of Spanish origin and lentil soups and stews are also prepared. Beans in general are drawn upon by vegetarians and by people who fast on religious holidays.

Frijoles Volteados (Guatemalan Thick Bean Puree)

1 1/2 cup boiled black or red beans, or one 15-ounce can	2 garlic cloves, minced
1 small onion, minced	2 TBSP oil or lard
	1/2 cup water
	1/2 tsp salt

If using canned beans, drain and rinse them before proceeding. Puree the beans in a blender or food processor with the water. Heat the oil or lard in a skillet over medium heat and sauté the onion and garlic for 3 minutes. Add the bean puree and add salt to taste. Cook, stirring occasionally, until the mixture is thick and it separates from the edges and bottom of the skillet. Serve with tortillas or rice.

CHILES

Chiles are indigenous to the Americas and their culinary use is nowhere as sophisticated as it is in México. In most of the world chiles have been embraced in the limited role of "heat" providers, but Mexican cuisine exploits the flavor and texture differences of the different chile varieties. Chiles can be used fresh or dried. When dried, the qualities of the chile change so much that the dry and fresh versions of the same chile are reserved for different culinary purposes. Each Latin American region has its own kinds of chile and they are generally not considered interchangeable. The word *chile* is used by Mexicans and Central Americans because it comes from the Nahuatl language, but the word *ají* that comes from Arawak languages is used in the Caribbean and some South American regions. The word *ají* is also used by South Americans to refer to hot sauces and dishes.

Fresh chiles give a distinctive fruity and hot taste to Latino dishes. Bell peppers have become common in Latino cooking to add color and chile taste to dishes without adding heat. Sometimes they are also used as a substitute for Italian frying peppers and for the sweet but flavorful *ajíes dulces* that are the base of the ground *sofrito* paste that flavors Caribbean cooking. Mildly hot serrano and jalapeño chiles are easily available in the United States and have become all-purpose chiles, although they often have almost no heat and little taste. The very hot habanero chile is also easy to find and it guarantees a hot and spicy meal. South American finger peppers, called *ají de montaña* or *ají entero*, are hot and fragrant and they are combined with herbs and onions to make table condiments. Peruvian and Bolivians buy imported *rocoto* or *locoto* peppers frozen or in brine. *Rocotos* are medium-sized round hot chiles that are yellow, brown, red, or orange when ripe. They are stuffed or used to flavor other dishes. Another important chile in Peruvian cuisine is *ají amarillo* (yellow chile), which is 3 to 4 inches long and has a golden yellow color and a hot and fruity taste. It is available frozen, dried, brined, and pureed, and it is indispensable to make the creamy potato salad *papas a la huancaína*, the seafood stew *cau cau*, and many other dishes. Brazilians use a hot chile called *malagueta* that is similar to Tabasco chiles; Colombians make salsa with a tiny, round, and very hot chile called *ají chivato*; and Guatemalans flavor many of their foods with *chiles guaques*. The fresh chiles most frequently used by Mexicans are *poblanos* and Anaheim (also known as *chile verde* or California green chiles). *Poblanos* are big, bright green, and mildly hot. They are used to make Mexican *chiles rellenos* (stuffed chiles) and the roasted strips called *rajas* that are used as a topping or condiment. They have become more easily available in recent years, bringing about a comeback of recipes that had become rare in their absence. Anaheim is one of the most widely used chiles among Mexican Americans and it is the green chile of Southwestern cuisine.

Peruvians use dried chiles like *ají limo* in sauces and *ceviches* (citrus-marinated raw seafood), and the very hot small chile called *hontaka*. Mexicans use a wide range of dried chiles. The New México red chile, or *chile colorado*, is mildly hot and it is used to make New Mexican chili powder. Other dried chiles that are mildly hot are roasted, soaked, and pureed to make the base of different kinds of salsas and *moles* (ground seed and chile sauces). Among them there are *ancho* and *mulato* chiles, which are dry poblano chiles with a red-black color and an earthy and fruity flavor. Other dry chiles used to make *moles* are the red and mild *guajillos* and the dark and wrinkled *pasillas* (literally "little raisins"). *Pasilla* chiles are the dried form of the *chilaca* chile. They have a complex flavor that is simultaneously mildly hot, sweet, and slightly bitter. They are hard to find and sometimes *ancho* chiles are mislabeled as *pasillas*. Another kind of dried chile used by Mexicans to make salsas and to flavor meatballs and other dishes is *chipotle*. These are smoke-dried *jalapeños* available dry and canned in *adobo* sauce. The very hot *piquín* and its wild cousin *chiltepín* are also widely used, particularly by Mexican Americans from Arizona and New México.

VEGETABLES

Greens

Latino cuisine features many cultivated greens like spinach and *acelgas* (Swiss chard), as well as wild greens like *verdolagas* (purslane) and *quelites* (lamb's quarters). *Verdolagas* are considered weeds in gardens but they have a mildly acidic taste that is prized by many Mexican Latinos. They can be eaten freshly picked in salads or lightly steamed. *Quelites* have a pungent taste similar to mustard greens and they should be lightly cooked until wilted.

Hearts of Palm

Called *palmitos* in Spanish, hearts of palm are the ivory-colored inner cylinders of the stem of palm trees. Their taste is similar to artichoke hearts and they are usually available canned. *Palmitos* are eaten raw in salads, cooked with rice, or prepared as filling for empanadas (turnovers).

Nopalitos

Nopalitos are the tender fleshy paddles of a young prickly pear cactus that are used cooked in salads. When cut into long strips they look and taste like green beans. They are available fresh and canned.

Okra

Okra, or *guingombó*, are long tapered green pods that were brought to the Americas from Africa. They have a gelatinous interior that thickens soups and stews. They are used in Brazilian and Caribbean cooking.

Pacaya

Pacayas are tender palm tree blossoms used in Central American cooking. In the United States they are available in jars. *Pacayas* are usually fried in egg batter or chopped to use in salads and fillings.

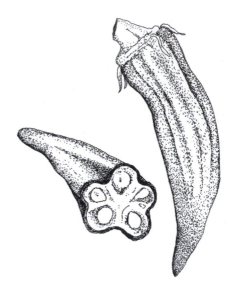

Okra. © J. Susan Cole Stone.

Squash/Pumpkin

Summer squashes like zucchinis are stuffed or added to salads and stews. Mexicans also use squash as an ingredient in their vegetable pickles. *Chayote* squash are avocado-shaped with a white or light green skin. The white flesh has a high water content and a delicate flavor. *Chayotes* can be stuffed or added to soups and stews. Winter squashes like pumpkin are used to prepare sweets, fritters, and cream soups. Colombians prepare savory tamales made with a pumpkin, potato, and *arepa* flour dough. Mexicans and Guatemalans use toasted ground squash seeds to make *moles* and *pepianes*, and also make elegant stuffed squash blossom dishes.

FRUIT

Eating fruit as breakfast, snack, and dessert is an important element of Latino food culture. In Latino neighborhoods ready-to-eat peeled and cut fruit is sold by street vendors, sometimes dressed with a little salt and chile powder. Bananas of different varieties are enjoyed unadorned. Mangoes, papayas, and pineapples are eaten fresh, maybe with a sprinkle of salt and chile. They have also become ingredients in innovative salsas and pickles. Fragrant pink-fleshed guavas are most likely enjoyed as a sweet red paste that is often paired with dulce de leche (caramelized milk) or with *queso blanco* (fresh cheese) for dessert. Guava paste is also used as a filling for pastries and turnovers. Citrus fruit like lime and sour Seville oranges are indispensable in *ceviches* and *adobos*. The orange juice and milk shake poetically known as *morir soñando* (literally "to die dreaming") is extremely popular. Mexicans make drinks called *aguas frescas* with all kinds of fresh fruit. A particularly colorful *agua fresca* is made with *tunas* (prickly pears), the sweet, bright pink-fleshed fruits of the nopal cactus. Tamarind, *maracuyá* (starfruit), the fragrant *mamey sapote*, sweet white-fleshed *guanábana* (soursop), *cherimoya* (custard apple), and other fruit are consumed fresh if possible but they are more readily available as canned juices, frozen pulp, and syrups. Frozen fruit pulp is blended with milk or water and sugar to make shakes called *batidos*, *batidas*, or *licuados* that are frequent meal accompaniments. Fruit syrups are used by street vendors in the summer to flavor snow cones called *piraguas* by Puerto Ricans and *frío frío* by Dominicans. More difficult-to-find fruit like *lulo* or *naranjilla*, *nance*, *jocote*, and *tomate de árbol* or *tamarillo* (tree tomato) are sought after by those who remember these and so many other fruits from their countries of origin. Fresh ones can be bought by mail with overnight delivery and some of them are available frozen.

Coconut is used in many sweet and savory dishes. In the Caribbean, Brazil, and all the coastal areas of Latin America with a strong African influence coconut milk and grated coconut give a distinctive character to many dishes. Coconuts are used to flavor tamales, *humitas*, rice pudding, bread pudding, ice cream, savory rice dishes, cakes, and flan (milk and egg custard). Hondurans from coastal regions often accompany their meals with *pan de coco* (coconut bread). South Americans make cream of coconut and shrimp soups. Brazilians make hominy and coconut pudding, and Colombians make a sweet yuca and coconut torte. Puerto Ricans, Cubans, and Dominicans make an incredible assortment of sweets that exploit the flavor and texture possibilities of coconut. Some feature the freshness of grated coconut while others take advantage of the intense flavor of toasted coconut. Drinks like *piña colada* and *coquito* (coconut and rum) take advantage of the smoothness and fragrance of coconut cream.

Tomatoes, *tomatillos*, and avocados are botanically classified as fruits although they are popularly considered as vegetables because they are used in savory rather than sweet preparations. Tomatoes are an indispensable ingredient in all Latino cooking. They provide the base for stews, soups, and salsas, and add to the flavor and color of yellow and red rice dishes. Tomatoes are also frequently used in salads and as a flavorful topping or garnish. *Tomatillos*, also known as husk tomatoes, are small vine fruit in the family of gooseberries. They have a papery green/brown husk and a sour taste and generally need to be cooked. Mexicans and Guatemalans use them for green salsas and *moles*. Avocados, best known in the form of Mexican guacamole, are frequently featured in other Latino meals simply sliced as an accompaniment to meats, salads, soups, and sandwiches. They are also pureed to make cream soups and sauces.

MEAT, POULTRY, AND SEAFOOD

Latino meals frequently feature meat, poultry, or seafood as a main dish. Beef is the meat of choice for Argentineans, Brazilians, Uruguayans, and Mexicans from northern México or the U.S. Southwest. *Carne seca*, also known as *tasajo* or beef jerky, was the base of many preparations that today are more commonly cooked using fresh meat. Depending on the cut, beef is fried, roasted, grilled, or stewed. It is used in soups and it is ground, cubed, or cut into strips to prepare stuffings for empanadas, fritters, tacos, and enchiladas. The famous South American *parrilladas* are different cuts of meat, sausages, and vegetables grilled together. Peruvians skewer marinated cubes of beef and beef hearts to make *anticuchos*. Goat meat is also appreciated, although it is not consumed as frequently. Roasted kid is a specialty of Mexicans in the Southwest and goat stews are favored by Dominicans and other Caribbean Latinos.

Pork is the most important meat for Caribbean and Andean Latinos. Roasted pork is the premier holiday dish for Cubans, Puerto Ricans, and Dominicans. Pork in Latino cooking is fried or stewed, and it is used to make stuffing for tacos, enchiladas, tamales, *arepas*, and empanadas. Seasoned ground pork is turned into sausages like *chorizo* and *longaniza*. Pork lard is used as a cooking medium and as an ingredient in the dough for tamales. Even though lard use has been reduced by Latinos, it is still used when the cook does not want to compromise the texture and taste of a favorite dish. Pork rind is also widely used as a seasoning in *pupusas*, *mofongo*, *mangú*, and rice dishes. Perfectly fried pork rind, called *chicharrón*, is occasionally served as a side dish and it is considered as irresistible as bacon. The tripe stew *mondongo* remains an important part of Caribbean Latino cuisine, although many Latinos reject any dishes made with organ meats. *Cuy*, or guinea pig, is sought after by Ecuadorians and other Latinos from the Andes.

Chicken and turkey are widely used and can often substitute for beef and pork in many dishes. Spicy marinated roasted chickens are a specialty of many Peruvian restaurants and of Latino fast-food chains like the Guatemalan *Pollo Campero*. Because freshness is highly valued and the mass-produced chickens available in supermarkets are generally bland and watery, many Latinos prefer to buy live chickens in *viveros* (live poultry shops) where they can choose the sex and age of their chicken and have it slaughtered to be cooked on the same day.

Fish and shellfish have an important role in the Latino cuisines that originate in coastal areas. Fish is generally baked or fried whole and served with a sauce. *Ceviches* and *tiraditos* in which strips or cubes of raw fish are served after a quick marinating in citrus juice and chile have been made popular by Peruvians, Ecuadorians, and Mexicans from Yucatán. Caribbean Latinos have a similar preparation called *escabeche* in which cooked fish is marinated in vinegar, olive oil, garlic, and black pepper. The salted and dried codfish called *bacalao* remains an important ingredient for many preparations of Spanish and Portuguese origin, as well as for the ubiquitous Caribbean codfish fritters. Clams, mussels, shrimp, crab, lobster, octopus, squid, and conch are enjoyed simply cooked and dressed or in *ceviches*, cocktails, and fish and seafood stews. Brazilians use dried shrimp whole or ground to flavor soups and stews.

Ceviche de Camarón (Ecuadorian Shrimp Ceviche)

2 dozen large shrimp, peeled
  and deveined
1 red onion, thinly sliced
1/2 cup freshly squeezed
  lime juice
1 tomato, chopped

1 jalapeño or serrano chile,
  seeded and finely chopped
1/4 cup coarsely chopped
  cilantro
1/4 tsp salt

Bring water to a rolling boil in a saucepan. Place the shrimp in the boiling water for 1 minute and quickly drain and rinse with cold water. Sprinkle the onions with salt and let stand for 15 minutes before rinsing the salt out. Mix all the ingredients in a glass or nonreactive bowl and refrigerate for 1 hour.

DAIRY PRODUCTS

Milk is consumed in fruit shakes called *batidos* and *licuados*. In the form of dulce de leche, *cajeta*, or *arequipe* (sweetened caramelized milk of thick consistency), it is dessert on its own or as a sauce or filling for crepes, cookies, and cakes. *Crema* is a pourable table cream similar to *crème fraîche* that is enjoyed as a topping on foods like tacos, enchiladas, and fried sweet plantains. Canned evaporated milk is sometimes added to coffee and to fruit shakes and it is one of the three kinds of milks in *pastel tres leches* (three milk cake).

Latino cooking uses a wide variety of fresh white semisoft cheeses made with cow's milk. Latino fresh cheeses are sometimes labeled *queso de hoja* (leaf cheese) because traditionally they were sold wrapped in banana leaves. The most widely used is *queso blanco*, a cheese that softens when heated but does not melt. It is used as stuffing or in the dough of *arepas* and yuca breads. Salvadorans use it for their quesadillas, which are sweet cheesecakes not to be confused with Mexican savory quesadillas that are tortillas stuffed with melting cheese. *Queso blanco* paired with sweet guava paste makes a classic dessert combination. *Queso fresco*, on the other hand, is salty and slightly acidic and it is widely used crumbled on top of dishes or as a filling. A variety of *queso fresco* popular with Mexican Latinos is called *panela*. Caribbean Latinos use *queso de freír*, a saltier and drier *queso fresco* that does not melt even when fried. The most popular melting cheeses are *asadero*, *Chihuahua*, and quesadilla, which are used in dishes where melting is desirable. *Cotija* or *añejo* is a dry and crumbly Mexican aged cheese that is sprinkled as a topping. *Queso de papa* is an orange-colored firm cheese similar to Colby that Caribbean Latinos use in fritters and for snacking. Goat cheeses and Argentine parmesan are other Latin American cheeses widely used in the United States. In spite of the increasing availability of all these products, sour cream, mozzarella, and parmesan cheese are often used instead of real *crema*, *queso fresco*, and *cotija*, respectively.

CONDIMENTS AND SEASONINGS

Latino cooking is well known for the tasty and colorful table sauces and spicy condiments that accompany all meals. Mexicans have an incredible variety of salsas that can be fresh or cooked, hot or mild. There are green salsas like *salsa verde* made with green chiles and tomatillos, and *chile verde* made with New Mexican green chiles. There are also red salsas like *salsa roja* made with pureed tomatoes, and the cooked tomato-based *salsa ranchera*. Raw salsas made with coarsely chopped ingredients like tomatoes, onions, cilantro, and chiles are known as *salsa cruda*, *pico de gallo*, or *salsa fresca*. Other salsas are named after the chiles used in them or after their intended use like *salsa taquera* (taco sauce). *Moles*, including *guacamole*, are also considered salsas because salsa in Spanish simply means sauce.

Other Latinos also have their distinctive sauces. Puerto Rican tables usually feature *pique*, a vinegar and hot chile sauce. There are commercial *pique* brands made with pureed chiles and vinegar, and homemade versions in which fresh chiles like habaneros sit in vinegar for the diner to choose whether to eat the chiles or just use the flavored vinegar. Another Puerto Rican condiment is called *ajilimójili*, which is made with garlic and sweet and hot peppers plus coriander, lime juice, and olive oil.

Andean hot chile table condiments are called *ajíes* and they vary from country to country. Peruvian *ají verde*, for example, is made with serrano chiles, cilantro, flat-leaf parsley, oregano, lime juice, olive oil, and garlic. This condiment is usually served with grilled meat or chicken. South

American *aliños* or *adobos* are milder condiments made with dried spices and herbs like granulated garlic, cumin, dried oregano, and annatto seeds. Other common South American table sauces are *Chimichurri, salsa rosada,* and *salsa de maní. Chimichurri* is the indispensable accompaniment to Argentine grilled meats. It is made with vinegar, fresh flat-leaf parsley, garlic, olive oil, dried oregano, and red pepper flakes. *Salsa rosada* (pink sauce) is a mayonnaise, ketchup, and bell pepper sauce that is used in lobster, shrimp, and crabmeat cold salads, and as a dip for vegetables. *Salsa de maní* is a peanut sauce flavored with scallions, cilantro, and hot peppers that is the classic accompaniment to many Ecuadorian and Peruvian dishes.

Pickled vegetables called *escabeches* or *encurtidos* are frequent table condiments. Pickled onions, carrots, and mixed vegetables often complete a Mexican meal. *Cebollas encurtidas,* red onions pickled in lemon juice and pepper, are a classic accompaniment to Ecuadorian *ceviches.* Salvadoran *pupusas* are always served with a shredded cabbage and carrot pickle called *curtido.* Cuban *mojo* is a citrus juice, olive oil, and garlic vinaigrette used both as a marinade and as a table sauce.

Latino cuisine makes extensive use of seasonings and marinades that are applied to meats and fish before cooking. The generic name *adobos* means different things in different countries. For Mexicans *adobo* is a pungent chile paste and for Argentineans, Uruguayans, and Brazilians it can mean a simple salt, pepper, and lemon juice marinade used to tenderize and to baste meat. Caribbean cooks apply a garlic, vinegar, black pepper, and oregano *adobo* to most meats, either freshly made or in the popular commercial powdered form.

Cooking fats can be lard or olive and other vegetable oils. These can be plain or colored with annatto seeds. Brazilians also make use of a red palm oil called *dendê* that gives a distinctive flavor to many dishes. Numerous Latino dishes are prepared with *sofrito,* which is a mixture of ground onions, garlic, bell peppers, tomato, and other ingredients. Each Latino cuisine has made its own adaptation of this Spanish-origin preparation. The Puerto Rican version of *sofrito* includes *ajíes dulces,* cilantro, and *recao* (long leaf cilantro). Sautéing *sofrito* in lard or oil is the first step in the preparation of soups, stews, beans, and rice dishes. Because it is so widely used, home cooks normally make large batches of *sofrito* to have enough to use throughout the week and to freeze some for later use. Commercially available *sofrito* is used when there is no time or ingredients to make it at home.

SPICES AND HERBS

While the use of hot chiles distinguishes Mexican and, to a lesser extent, Andean cuisines, other Latino cuisines like Puerto Rican, Cuban, Dominican,

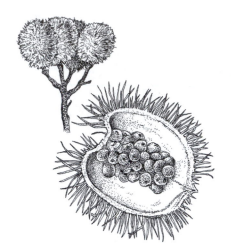

Achiote (annatto). © J. Susan Cole Stone.

and Argentinean make limited use of hot chiles, relying more on garlic, herbs, and spices. Oregano, flat-leaf parsley, cilantro, bay leaf, cumin, garlic, and black pepper are the most commonly used seasonings in Latino cuisine. The distinctive taste of Caribbean cooking in great part depends on *recao*, a long narrow leaf with jagged edges also known as *culantro*. Its aroma and flavor is similar to cilantro but it is much stronger. An herb favored by Mexicans and Central Americans is the strongly aromatic and slightly bitter *epazote* (pigweed). This herb is a must in the preparation of beans because it is reputed to prevent flatulence. Salvadorans use the pungent flower *loroco*, particularly in cheese *pupusas* and pickled. Colombians season *ajiaco* (chicken, maize, and potato stew) with the herb *guascas*, and Peruvians and Bolivians flavor many traditional Andean dishes with the herbs *huacatay* (black mint) and *quilquiña*. Some Latino desserts are scented with orange blossom water.

A widely used spice is *achiote* seeds (annatto), used to give color to all kinds of dishes. Caribbean cooks heat up the seeds in oil or lard, and then drain them out and use the resulting red fat to cook. It is also used in powdered form usually marketed as *Bijol*. Ground annatto seeds are the base of some Yucatecan seasoning pastes. Spices other than annatto, black pepper, and cumin are generally reserved for sweet dishes and the most common are cinnamon, cloves, anise seed, star anise, and vanilla.

BEVERAGES

Nonalcoholic

The repertoire of drinks in Latino food culture is vast. Fruit-based beverages include freshly made or canned juices as well as fruit drinks like *batidos* and *aguas frescas*. Maize-based drinks or *atoles* can be flavored with fruits or with chocolate, in which case it is called *champurrado*. A drink popular in New México is *pinole*, made with roasted cornmeal or wheat flavored with milk, sugar, and spices. Thick hot chocolate made by melting plain or sweetened chocolate tablets is enjoyed at breakfast or as a part of a light supper. Aloe juice and infusions made from chamomile flowers and other herbs are enjoyed as drinks and as medicinal aids. Sweetened oatmeal drinks sometimes mixed with fruit juices can be served as dessert or as breakfast, particularly for children. They can be homemade but there is a wide variety of mixes and ready-made oatmeal drinks available. Ecuadorians call these drinks *cuáker* after the popular Quaker brand oats. Another popular children's beverage is Milo, a Nestle brand powdered chocolate and malt mix that is prepared with cold or hot milk. *Horchata* is a refreshing drink made with ground rice, almonds, or almost any other seed and flavored with sugar and cinnamon. Breakfast beverages for adults include strong coffee and, in the case of many South Americans, *mate*. The infusion made with *mate* leaves is drunk from a hollowed gourd with a metal straw. In many cases coffee is also served after meals, even in the evening. Mexican Latinos sometimes prepare *café de olla*, which is coffee cooked in a pot flavored with unrefined sugar and cinnamon.

Many Latinos drink carbonated beverages, including both U.S. and imported brands. Certain soda varieties and flavors are imported from Latin America because they have a loyal following in the United States. A carbonated nonalcoholic malt beverage called *malta* is imported from the Caribbean. A popular soda reminiscent of cream soda is *cola champagne*, which comes in different brands from different countries. Sodas made from the stimulant berry called *guaraná* have both Latino and non-Latino fans. There are also coconut, apple, and pineapple sodas available. *Inca Cola* has a strong following among Peruvians and other South Americans. Aside from the variety of flavors, one reason why imported sodas remain so popular is because many are still manufactured with cane sugar instead of corn syrup, which gives them a different taste.

Alcoholic

Beer is one of the alcoholic drinks most widely enjoyed by Latinos. Many people prefer the brands from their countries of origin so there is a wide range of Latin American beers available in Latino markets. Among the most popular are *Negra Modelo*, *Corona*, and *Sol* from México; *Pilsener* and *Club* from Ecuador; *Presidente* and *Quisqueya Extra* from the Dominican Republic; and *Aguila* and *Club Colombia* from Colombia. While Mexicans often drink their beer with a slice of lime, Colombians sometimes mix it with *cola champagne* to create the refreshing drink called *refajo*. Slightly alcoholic drinks made with fermented maize, yuca, or fruits are generically known as *chicha*. Wine is most commonly consumed as sangría. Although many Latinos are wine connoisseurs, wine drinking is not part of the wider Latino culture, except for those from wine-producing countries like Chile and Argentina.

One of the most recognizable Latino distilled alcohols is rum, which is made from sugarcane molasses or juice and is aged in oak barrels. Rum is used in cocktails like *piña colada*, daiquirí, *Cuba libre*, and *mojito*. It is also used to make Christmas drinks like the fruity Mexican *ponche de Navidad* and the Puerto Rican coconut and rum drink called *coquito*. Brazilian *cachaça* is distilled from sugarcane juice and it is the base of the cocktail called *caipirinha*. A brandy distilled from grapes in Perú, Chile, and Bolivia is *pisco* and it is served in cocktails like *pisco sour*.

A traditional alcoholic drink from Mesoamerica is *pulque*, which is the fermented juice of the maguey or agave succulent plant. *Mezcal* is a distilled spirit from the same plant, and tequila is a specific kind of *mezcal* made from the blue agave plant in the region of Jalisco in México. White or silver tequila is not aged and it is used in cocktails like margarita. Tequilas labeled *reposado*, *añejo*, and *extra añejo* are aged in oak barrels for a minimum of 3 months, 1 year, and 3 years, respectively. These fine tequilas have a darker color and are served neat or accompanied by a shot of spicy *sangrita* made with orange juice, tomato juice, and chiles.

3

Cooking

WHO DOES THE COOKING?

In the United States, as well as in Latin America, cooking at home has traditionally been the responsibility of women. In Latino homes women are generally in charge of the kitchen, although cooking duties are often shared with other household members. Assimilation and migration conditions have created new types of Latino households and eating establishments that are different from Latin American ones. In such settings Latino cooking is developing its own distinctive character.

One of the dominant Latino household patterns is the nuclear family headed by two parents or female-headed. In these families it is still common for the mother to do most of the cooking, sometimes alternating with the husband or with the children. Like all families, Latino families have different ways of sharing cooking tasks.

Another common household pattern, particularly among recent immigrants, is sharing a house or apartment with relatives and/or nonrelatives. In these households people often cook together in shifts. On Sundays and on special occasions large batches of food are cooked and shared by all members of the household. Salvadorans in Long Island, for example, improvise a barbecue or a *sancocho* (meat and vegetable stew) to feed Sunday visitors.[1] Women are more likely to cook together on Sundays and holidays when there is more time to cook festive dishes that require special skills that the men are less likely to have.

Making a *sancocho*. Courtesy of Douglas Gómez.

Another kind of household is composed of migratory workers who live isolated in labor camps and have limited income and cooking facilities. Most of these workers live in poverty and few of them receive the food assistance for which they qualify. Low income and lack of transportation to grocery stores affect the way they cook and eat. They tend to cook less at home and depend more on cheap fast foods, but when they do cook, women and men tend to share the work equally.[2]

Outside of the household, women cook for single men in contexts that range from regularly sharing home-cooked meals with friends or relatives, to pushcarts and small restaurants that cater to workers of one or more Latino nationality. Many such restaurants operate as *fondas* in which only one or two prix-fixe specials are available each day. While cooking is generally considered an unfair burden on women, many Latinas see cooking outside of the home as a way to assert their agency and economic independence. Men also cook outside of the household in restaurant kitchens of all sizes and cooking all kinds of cuisines, although few have had the opportunity of becoming chefs. Still, many men have acquired cooking skills in their jobs that have made them less dependent on women for their basic food needs.

The reasons why people cook go beyond the biological need for food. For Latinos, cooking the food of their countries of origin becomes a way to affirm their cultural identity and their family history. Cooking with or for other Latinos at home is a way of creating networks of solidarity that function as an extended family. Small Latino restaurants are not only places to eat; they are also a space where Latino ways of socialization and entertainment find a space outside of the home. Individuals can find reliable home-style cooking while watching a soccer game or enjoying Spanish-language television and music. On Sundays whole families dress up and go out together for dinners at restaurants that sometimes offer live music. Some restaurants serve actively as cultural brokers by providing a space for cultural and literary events, and for meetings to discuss community and political issues. Restaurants create and strengthen communities by providing continuity with the culinary traditions of Latin American countries while at the same time helping to negotiate the changes brought about in the United States. They are also sites for cultural exchange where Latinos from different backgrounds become acquainted with each other's food, fueling the creativity that is behind pan-Latino cuisine. Finally, cooking in Latino restaurants is also a way for people to serve as cultural ambassadors insofar as they represent and translate Latino cuisines and cultures for the larger non-Latino community.

BETWEEN ANGLO AMERICAN AND LATIN AMERICAN COOKING

There is no unified Latin American cuisine and there are no unified national cuisines either since there are as many differences inside the countries as there are between them. Latin American cuisines are the result of centuries of fusion of many cuisines of the world so they should not be conceived as a single, static, pure or authentic cuisine against which Latino cuisine can be measured. Latino cooking in the United States is not only as diverse as the different Latin American countries and regions, but also as diverse as their migration histories. Latino cuisine is only the latest chapter in the long history of culinary fusions in the Americas.

When analyzing Latino culture in general, scholars usually debate whether the balance between Latin American and U.S. cultures is one in which Latin American culture is bound to gradually disappear because of acculturation and assimilation. Latinos in this case are seen as in the process of losing their Latin American culture as they acquire the Anglo American one. A different position sees the relationship between the two cultures as transculturation, a process in which a third culture is created. Like Spanglish, the Latino language that combines English and Spanish, Latino cuisine is a new cuisine that is more than the sum of Latin American and mainstream U.S. cuisines. It is the ongoing result of modifying and combining both cuisines in the process of creating a new cuisine that is in turn affecting both Latin American and U.S. cuisines. U.S. food culture has been deeply marked by Latinos, from the creation of Southwestern cuisine to the mainstream character of salsa, tortilla wraps, and Cuban sandwiches. Latin American food culture has also incorporated many Latino foods, as Tex-Mex restaurants in México testify.

Latino cooking exists in a continuum between Latin American and Anglo American cuisines. The full range of positions in the continuum can be witnessed, from people who cook much in the same way as in Latin America to those who do not cook Latin American food at all. Most Latinos are somewhere in the middle, alternating and combining both kinds of cooking and ultimately creating their own.

In some households, regional cooking traditions are conserved with relatively few changes. Some migrants live in neighborhoods that are extensions of their villages back home and socialize almost exclusively among themselves. This is generally the case among indigenous people from southern México like the Zapotecs who, in response to the racist disdain with which they are generally treated, have little contact with other Mexicans and with Anglo Americans. On Sundays, usually the only day of the week in which they do not work, they visit each other to share food and drink and to talk about life and politics in the United States and back home. Zapotecs in Los Angeles, for example, serve visitors mostly Oaxacan dishes like *mole* (chicken in a sauce made with ground nuts and chiles) and *cecina* (grilled, chile paste–marinated leg of pork).[3]

On the other side of the spectrum there are middle-class Latinos who live scattered all over the United States. They do not live in Latino neighborhoods and often have married non-Latinos. Many of them come from the urban middle classes of their countries of origin and as such are used to a cosmopolitan way of cooking and eating in which Latin American regional and national cuisines coexist and sometimes are subordinated to international trends. In the United States they can continue their cosmopolitan food habits and develop them further due to the wide range of international ingredients and cuisines available in the United States.

The cooking habits of the majority of Latinos lie in between the two extremes and they are very flexible. When Latinos cook mainstream U.S. foods like hamburgers, hot dogs, steak, and pasta they usually add flavorings like garlic, chile, salsa, and other condiments. Latinos regularly prepare the basic Latin American foods that they are familiar with like tortillas in the Mexican case and rice and beans in the case of Caribbean Latinos. Mexican Latinos use factory-made maize tortillas for daily consumption and use *masa harina* (instant dried and powdered dough made with nixtamalized maize) to make tamales, but for a special treat or on special occasions they make fresh *masa* (dough made with freshly ground nixtamalized maize) from scratch for tortillas and tamales. Similarly, many Caribbean Latinos have adopted canned beans for convenience but prefer to boil dry beans at home whenever they can. All Latino recipes seem to have at least two versions: the traditional, labor- or time-intensive way and the faster, more convenient way. The first one yields the best results but it is not practiced as often as the second one. The time-saving way of cooking, which generally implies the use of electric appliances and the use of processed foods, is associated with life in the United States, although this way of cooking is also prevalent in urban centers in Latin America. Latino cuisine is neither Latin American nor Anglo American, but both. It can be argued that it might become the cuisine of America as a single continent stretching from north to south, overcoming the socio-linguistic boundaries inherited from colonial and imperial history.

CHANGE AND CONTINUITY

Several elements explain why Latino cuisine shows such a strong continuity with Latin American cooking: the increasingly wider availability of Latin American ingredients in the United States, the constant influx of new immigrants, the translocal quality of migration, and the need to assert identity and dignity in often racist and denigrating contexts.

Until a few decades ago, Latino cuisine had limited possibilities of existence in the United States. Many dishes were impossible to reproduce because they depended on ingredients that were not available or that were either not fresh enough or too expensive. Now ingredients that used to be rare are easily available, like plantains, yuca, and poblano chiles. Food marketers have noticed the steady increase of the Latino population and are eager to cater to them. Latino and non-Latino food companies are constantly expanding their inventory of Latino ingredients and have become more sensitive to regional differences. Goya Foods, traditionally associated with Caribbean products, now includes Mexican, Central American, and South American ingredients. Large supermarket chains constantly increase the space dedicated to Latino ingredients in an effort to attract Latino customers that still prefer to shop in neighborhood markets. The Internet and fast mail delivery have made even rare ingredients available, although at a high price. This increased availability of ingredients guarantees the viability of Latino cuisine.

Constant new migration from Latin America also helps to ensure continuity between Latin American and Latino cooking. People coming from diverse countries and regions renew the cooking knowledge and compensate for the loss of traditional culinary knowledge that is common among second- and third-generation Latinos. The concentration of Latino populations in certain areas also makes it possible to sustain markets and restaurants that cater to their food culture. Latino migration is considered translocal because of its constant flow between two or more countries. Translocal communities have strong ties and community influence in both countries and serve as negotiators between the two cultures. Translocal migration allows for Latino cooking habits to have frequent contact with Latin American ones, thus blurring the sharp lines that might have differentiated them otherwise.

The need to assert identity and dignity in the racist and denigrating contexts faced by many Latinos also explains why Latino cooking remains close to Latin American traditions. For example, south Texas Mexicans affirm their continuity with the ranching culture of northern México when they get together to cook *barbacoa de cabeza* (pit-roasted cow head including brains, tongue, and eyes).[4] This food is rejected by outsiders but south Texas Mexicans have transformed it into a badge of identity. *Barbacoa de cabeza*, unlike tacos and enchiladas, is a dish that is theirs only and that only they know how to value. Similarly, there are other dishes that are used as identity markers because they are likely to be rejected by outsiders, either because they are considered bland like root vegetables or because they use tripe and other organ meats that are not used in mainstream cooking in the United States. Cooking such foods reinforces the Latino sense of identity and self-worth that sometimes feels threatened. Even though dishes that are rejected by outsiders constitute a small part of Latino cuisine, the effort to preserve them is a way in which Latinos assert that Latino cuisine should be defined by Latinos instead of by mainstream U.S. culture.

Even though the continuity between Latino and Latin American cooking is remarkable, Latino cuisine is the result of important changes imposed by different social, economic, and ecologic conditions in the United States. Important changes are the result of circumstances such as long work hours and low income; limited availability of fresh, local, homegrown, or wildly gathered ingredients; the need to adapt Latino cuisine to suit the taste of U.S.-born children and non-Latino spouses; the clash with mainstream U.S. food culture; and the cultural exchange with other Latinos and non-Latinos.

Most Latinos have low-paying jobs that require long work hours. Limited income means that much Latino cooking is guided by the need to economize. Inferior ingredients and processed foods have an important role in much Latino cuisine, making it closer to working-class U.S. cooking than to Latin American cuisines. Ground meat and canned vegetables take the place of fresh meat and vegetables. A common complaint among recent Latino immigrants is that they eat worse in the United States than in their countries of origin. One reason for this is the lack of fresh ingredients that can be procured without money in rural Latin America if one grows them or gathers them from the wild. Homegrown foods include tomatoes, maize, chiles, and cilantro in México and bananas, plantains, and fruits in the Caribbean. Food growing and gathering in U.S. cities is more difficult if not impossible. Lack of land to grow food and lack of areas from which one can gather wild foods means relying on packaged foods from the supermarket or on less-expensive processed foods. Latino immigrants have more money to buy food in the United States than they did in their villages but the food that they can buy is often of inferior quality than what they can get in Latin America. Even in the case of affluent Latinos, many of the ingredients that they can buy are considered different and often unsatisfactory. South American Latinos, for example, always miss the high-quality meats from their countries and consider that it is the meat itself that gives their dishes their distinctive flavor.

Latino cooking also becomes different from Latin American cuisines as people adapt traditional dishes to the taste of U.S.-born Latinos and of non-Latino spouses. U.S.-born Latino children often reject the food of their parents in favor of the foods that are consumed by their friends at school, while non-Latino spouses tend to embrace Latino cooking only partially. Latina mothers and wives in this situation have devised ways to feed their families by seasoning mainstream U.S. foods with Latino flavors or by preparing only Latino dishes that are not too challenging for their palates.

Many Latin American cooking practices that have clashed with mainstream U.S. culture have been substituted by more acceptable ones. Latino cuisine has been chastised for its use of lard and for its extensive repertoire of fried foods. Following mainstream dietary guidelines, many Latinos have abandoned the use of lard and reduced the preparation of fried foods. Latinos also have a preference for fresh eggs and freshly slaughtered chickens that they are used to raising at home, but this practice is not possible in the urban U.S. context. Some Latino neighborhoods feature *viveros* (live poultry shops) that sell all kinds of live poultry, from hens and capons to ducks, pheasants, pigeons, and guinea hens, but they face constant opposition from neighbors and health department regulations. Cooking food in pits is another Latino cooking practice that is reduced by the lack of land in which to do it and by some local health ordinances that prohibit it. Some regulations have also discouraged cooking with fresh blood, which is used to make blood sausages and other dishes.

Another important factor that explains the difference between Latino and Latin American cooking is the creativity fueled by the practice of cross-cultural eating that is prevalent in Latino neighborhoods shared by Latinos of different nationalities. Daily life in such neighborhood offers plenty of opportunities for cultural exchange. Neighborhood markets, food stalls, and restaurants allow Latinos of different nationalities and other ethnic groups to easily sample each other's foods. Ingredients and recipes from a great variety of traditions find their way into the kitchen where they are adapted and reinvented. Latinos in the United States are more aware of Latin American culinary diversity than Latin Americans. For example, Puerto Ricans living on the island generally may not know what Colombian *arepas* (maize griddle cakes) and Salvadoran *pupusas* (stuffed tortillas) are, but they are familiar and beloved foods of many New York Puerto Ricans. Latino cooking is a pan–Latin American cuisine created in the United States.

COOKBOOKS

The Latino cookbook market is extremely varied. Different kinds of cookbooks target different audiences and create and represent the Latino community in their own way. The wide variety of Latino cookbooks offers a window into the great diversity of the Latino population and into how a pan-Latino identity is being simultaneously created and contested. Spanish-language bookstores sell imported books that focus on the cuisines of Latin America. This kind of cookbook is bought by Latinos who want an authoritative reference to the cuisine of their countries, and they use it to recreate dishes that they remember but that they do not necessarily know how to make. There is also a constantly expanding number of cookbooks published in English that focus on Latin American cuisine in general and on individual national cuisines. These books serve as an introduction for non–Latin Americans and for second- and third-generation Latinos that are unfamiliar with their culinary heritage. A few bilingual cookbooks have been published, like *The Hispanic American Cookbook* (1985) by Nilda Luz Rexach, which was one of the first attempts to present a unified Latino cuisine, although its recipes are mostly Puerto Rican. The cookbooks that focus on Latino cooking as different from Latin American are relatively recent, ranging from large trade publications to small press and community cookbooks.

Many trade press cookbooks focus on a single Latino nationality, and they are intended to present Latino home cooking as opposed to both traditional Latin American cooking and to upscale Latino restaurant cuisine. These books are published in English often with a liberal use of words and phrases in Spanish. The shift from Spanish to an accented English is reflective of the unique identity of the cuisine asserting itself. Books like *Cocina de la familia: More Than 200 Authentic Recipes from Mexican American Home Kitchens* (1997) by Marilyn Tausend and Miguel Ravago, *Puerto Rican Cuisine in America: Nuyorican and Bodega Recipes* (1993) by Oswald Rivera, and *A Taste of Cuba: Recipes from the Cuban American Community* (1991) by Linette Creen and Felipe Rojas-Lombardi present Mexican, Puerto Rican, and Cuban cuisines, respectively, in the way in which they are practiced in the United States, using available ingredients and easily mastered techniques. These books have the intention of passing on in writing the adapted and new culinary knowledge from one generation to the next, and they also represent Latinos to a larger audience.

Other cookbooks focus on a specific Latino neighborhood or area. Many books focus on the cuisine of the border between the United States and México, like *The Border Cookbook: Authentic Home Cooking of the American Southwest and Northern México* (1995) by Cheryl Alters Jamison, and *Aprovecho: A Mexican American Border Cookbook* (2004) by Teresa Cordero Cordell and Robert Cordell. These books consider the culinary cultures of northern México and the Southwestern United States as a single culture that blurs the border. There are also a few cookbooks that compile recipes from urban neighborhoods with large Latino populations like *The Bronx Cookbook* (1997), by Gary Hermalyn and Peter Derrick, and *The Brooklyn Cookbook* (1991) by Lyn Stallworth and Rod Kennedy Jr. In these books Mexican and Puerto Rican recipes appear alongside African American, Chinese, German, Irish, Italian, Jewish, and Korean ones. The cuisine of Latinos in multiethnic neighborhoods is enriched with contact with many national cuisines but conserves its distinctiveness.

Community cookbooks, usually published for fundraising, feature the recipes of a specific locality. *Sabores de México* (2007), for example, is a bilingual collection of recipes collected by the Women's Collaborative for Health and Nutrition in rural Plumas County, California. This group of Mexican American women raises funds for health-related projects to benefit the Latino community. Similarly, *La cocina de la familia* (1998) is a collection of recipes from the people in the drug rehabilitation center *La bodega de la familia* in Alphabet City in the Lower East Side of Manhattan, New York. Books like these represent the community to the outside world and also help strengthen the ties within the community by creating a common identity.

A large number of the cookbooks devoted to Latino cuisine gather representative dishes from each Latino nationality to form the collage that is pan-Latino cuisine. The most popular is Daisy Martínez's *Daisy Cooks! Latin Flavors That Will Rock Your World* (2005), although Aarón Sánchez's *La comida del barrio: Latin-American Cooking in the U.S.A.* (2003) and *Our Latin Table: Celebrations, Recipes and Memories* (2003) by Fernando Saralegui and others are also good examples. These books combine homestyle recipes from different Latino backgrounds, but the authors are careful to specify what the origin of each recipe is. While creating a canon of pan-Latino recipes, books like these do not erase the distinctiveness of the different Latino cultures. Not only do they introduce Latino cuisines to outsiders, but they also introduce different Latinos to each other's cuisine.

Other cookbooks, like *Steven Raichlen's Healthy Latin Cooking* (1998) by Steven Raichlen and *Latina Lite Cooking* (1998) by María Dolores Beatriz, modify pan-Latino cuisine to accommodate current prescriptions for weight control and other health concerns. Yet another trend in pan-Latino cookbooks puts emphasis on food presentation to make it more suitable for entertaining like *Latin Chic: Entertaining with Style and Sass* (2005) by Carolina Buia and Isabel González and *Viva la Vida: Festive Recipes for Entertaining Latin-Style* (2002) by Rafael Palomino, Arlen Gargagliano, and Susie Cushner. Another upscale version of pan-Latino cuisine, which is best known as Nuevo Latino, was popularized by chefs Norman Van Aken and Douglas Rodríguez.

NUEVO LATINO

Latino cuisine is known predominantly in its working-class version. Latino restaurants are mostly neighborhood establishments serving economic home-style food. Mexican cuisine is becoming the exception because now there are upscale Mexican restaurants in cities all over the United States that serve a variety of regional Mexican dishes. It took Mexican cuisine very long to achieve this status in the United States and still people see Mexican Latino cuisine as closer to Taco Bell and Tex-Mex restaurants than to fine dining. The most widely recognized upscale version of Latino cuisine is only a few decades old and it started in Florida. It has a Cuban rather than a Mexican accent because, even though Mexicans are a larger and older migration, Cubans in Florida have a higher socioeconomic status than any other Latino community and they were able to sustain and create a more sophisticated cuisine, drawing from their Spanish and Caribbean heritage and from other Latino traditions.

The creation of Nuevo Latino cuisine as a restaurant cuisine that uses Latino ingredients and French technique is usually attributed to a group of chefs nicknamed the "Mango Gang," including Norman Van Aken, Douglas Rodríguez, Alan Susser, and Mark Militello, among others. These chefs decided to make use of the wealth of ingredients and culinary traditions that coexist in Florida to create a cuisine that has been known as "New World Cuisine," "Floribbean Cuisine," "Nuevo Cubano Cuisine," and "Nuevo Latino Cuisine." *Nuevo Latino* is the label that stuck and now this trend is present in New York City and other cities all over the country. While many people have welcomed Nuevo Latino restaurants, many Latinos are often disappointed by their dishes because they find that they have better presentation but are not as good in flavor as the traditional versions. According to its detractors, Nuevo Latino is the appropriation of the emerging pan-Latino cuisine to cater to the current taste paradigms of fine dining in the United States, just like Tex-Mex cuisine was the result of the appropriation of Mexican cuisine to cater to mainstream U.S. taste. More positively, it could be argued that Nuevo Latino cuisine has been only a starting point that created a space for Latinos to elaborate the high end of their cuisine, according to their own taste.[5]

COOKING TECHNIQUES

Latinos depend more on the senses than on measuring and timing as cooking guidelines. Latino culinary knowledge has not been systematically standardized in writing and recipes. People have learned to cook by cooking with more experienced cooks, not by reading cookbooks. A cook can tell by the smell when chiles and spices have been roasted enough. This is more efficient than timing because roasting for 30 seconds can be too little or too long depending on how dry the specific chiles or spices already are. Touch tells the cook if dough needs more or less water, taste helps adjust the level of acidity to compensate for the variability between one lime and another, and sight confirms when a food has been cooked to perfection. Only now that younger generations of Latinos have not grown up acquiring this kind of sensory knowledge in the kitchen has the need to try to capture it in written form arisen. In spite of many changes in traditional cooking methods, Latinos are still more likely than non-Latinos to cook meals from scratch.

Many of the techniques used in Latino kitchens are common to all cuisines while others are specific to a tradition or to a type of dish. Frying, boiling, and baking are commonly used techniques. Frying snacks and appetizers to a nongreasy golden crispness is a highly valued skill that does not generally depend on electric deep fryers. Boiling is important for beans, soups, and stews. Tamales require steaming and also some skill to wrap them because different varieties of tamales require their own wrapping technique. Proper wrapping provides an attractive presentation, plus it ensures that the tamales will acquire the right shape and that the filling will be totally encased in the dough. In the case of Puerto Rican *pasteles* (plantain and root vegetable tamales), adequate wrapping ensures that they will not get waterlogged when boiled. Another technique that is widely used is *baño de María* or cooking in a water bath. This is indispensable to make a smooth flan, the iconic Latino milk-and-egg custard dessert. Baking is used for breads and cakes, although many people prefer to buy them at *panaderías* and *reposterías* (bakeries and pastry shops) rather than make them at home.

Baking and oven roasting has become a frequent substitute for the important practice of wood fire roasting and grilling. Caribbean Latinos cherish the taste of a whole pig on a stick slowly roasted over a fire. Latinos from Argentina, Uruguay, Chile, and Paraguay favor *asados* (roasted beef) and *parrilladas*, which is different cuts of meat, sausages, and organ meats cooked on a spit over an open fire or on a grill. Brazilians call a similar mixed grill *churrasco*, although the same word in other countries refers to specific cuts of beef and not to the way of cooking them. Many Latinos also enjoy pit roasting or *barbacoa*. Mexican Americans in the Southwestern United States wrap meat in burlap and bury it in a pit with mesquite wood embers covered with

Argentine *parrillada*, New York. Courtesy of Cecilia Fonseca.

agave leaves. All these techniques can collectively be called *barbecue*, and indeed both the practice and the name were adopted and spread by Europeans who learned it from the Arawak Indians. However, because currently the word *barbecue* refers primarily to the charcoal grill common in U.S. backyards, Latinos resist applying the term to their *asados, parrilladas, churrascos,* and *barbacoas*. The taste, texture, and aroma produced by these techniques cannot be replicated by the oven or by charcoal or gas grills that people use as substitutes, particularly in urban settings. This explains why Latinos insist on using wood fire whenever possible.

Mexican American cooking follows many traditional Mexican techniques. Ingredients like onions, garlic, tomatoes, tomatillos, and chiles are roasted until they get black spots to concentrate the flavor and to give salsas a smoky taste. Roasting is traditionally done with an *asador*, a wire-mesh grill used to hold ingredients over a fire, but it is also done on a *comal* (griddle) or on a baking sheet under the broiler. Cooking with dry chiles requires quite a few steps that must be executed carefully in order to maximize their taste without ruining them. Dry chiles have to be cleaned and roasted before they are soaked, pureed, and strained to be used in salsas, *moles,* and other dishes. If the chiles are roasted for too long, they get a charred taste, and if they are soaked for too long or in water that is too hot, their flavor is gone. Extreme care also needs to be paid to the preparation of sauces like *mole*. The pureed ingredients for the sauce are added to very hot oil so it sizzles and boils immediately. The sauce base is stirred as it fries until it becomes a thick mass. Stock

Comal. © J. Susan Cole Stone.

is added and the sauce is allowed to simmer for a couple of hours to allow the flavors to develop. Poaching is another technique used in Mexican cooking. Poaching chicken in water with onions, garlic, carrots, and bay leaves produces juicy chicken for tacos and enchiladas plus a savory broth that is used to make soups and sauces. Rendering lard at home is an important technique because it yields a healthier and more flavorful lard than the hydrogenated commercially available variety. To render lard, pork fat is ground or finely chopped and cooked on a baking pan in a slow oven for about 30 minutes. The melted fat is strained and allowed to cool before it is stored in jars.

The preparation of maize for tortillas, *pupusas*, and tamales depends on nixtamalization. When instant dough like *masa harina* is not used, maize has to be boiled and soaked in a water and *cal* (slaked-lime) solution. The nixtamalized maize is then ground using a manual rotary grinder to make *masa* (dough). Patting *masa* to make tortillas is an art that requires years of practice so most Mexicans use a tortilla press. Salvadorans still stuff and pat their *pupusas* by hand since it yields a better result than sandwiching a filling between two tortillas and it is actually faster if one has mastered the technique.

Sautéing *sofrito* (ground ingredients like onions, tomatoes, garlic, and pepper) in olive oil or lard is the first step in the preparation of beans, soups, stews, and rice dishes. The combination of ingredients varies according to the dish, the region, and the cook. The distinctive flavor of Puerto Rican and other Caribbean cuisines comes from a *sofrito* of onions, garlic, *ajíes dulces* (sweet chiles), *culantro* (long leaf cilantro), tomatoes, and salted pork or cured ham. Caribbean Latinos are unlikely to cook any meat without seasoning it first. They use *adobo* to prepare most meats, whether it is going to be fried, grilled, or added to stews or rice. A basic *adobo* consists of ground garlic, black pepper, oregano, salt, and vinegar or lime juice. Ideally the meat is allowed to marinate in the *adobo* overnight in the refrigerator to allow its flavor to impregnate the meat.

A distinctive technique of Latino cuisine that comes from the Pacific coast of Latin America but has become a pan-Latino staple is *ceviche.* The basic *ceviche* technique consists of marinating raw pieces of fish in citrus juice and chile until the acid gives the fish an opaque, cooked appearance. There are endless *ceviche* ingredient combinations, including conch, octopus, shrimp, avocado, and coconut, but they all depend on the same basic procedure. A similar technique is *escabeche,* in which vegetables or cooked fish are marinated in vinegar with other seasonings.

Latino cooking pays attention to garnishing even for daily meals. Chopped vegetables are served both as complements to the dish and as garnishes that appeal to the eye. The accompaniment is an integral part of the dish and many dishes call for specific garnishes. Common Mexican garnishes include chopped onions, sliced radishes, chopped lettuce, and sliced lemons. Caribbean Latinos call their accompaniments *guarnición,* and they include strips of roasted bell peppers and pimento-stuffed olives. A dish is not considered complete without the finishing touch.

EQUIPMENT

The equipment used in Latino cooking is a combination of traditional manual tools and electric equipment. In some cases electric equipment has totally eliminated the use of a manual tool but generally people choose to use the electric substitute on a daily basis, reserving the manual tool for special occasions. The reason for this is that even though using traditional equipment

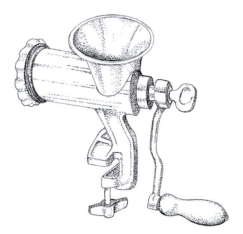

Rotary grinder. © J. Susan Cole Stone.

tends to be more labor-intensive, it is considered to yield a superior result in most cases.

The best example of a tool that has been practically abandoned in Latino cooking is the pre-Hispanic *metate*, which has been an essential tool in México and Central America for centuries. This flat volcanic grind stone is used with a stone pestle to pulverize seeds and spices and to grind maize to make *masa*. Few Latinos have the skill necessary to effectively grind seeds and spices on the *metate* so they use a coffee grinder or food processor for this task. The grinding of maize for *masa* is too laborious in the *metate* and most people find that a manual rotary grinder yields good results. Hand-cranked *molinos* (grinders) that can be attached to any countertop are made of cast iron and are inexpensive. The Mexican volcanic stone mortar and pestle, called *molcajete*, is used to puree ingredients for salsas. Electric blenders and food processors are used to make salsas but many cooks prefer the *molcajete* because it extracts more flavor from the ingredients and produces salsas with better texture.

Caribbean Latinos use a wooden mortar and pestle (*pilón y maceta*) to prepare the ingredients for *sofrito* and to make *mofongo* (Puerto Rican ground fried plantain dish) and *mangú* (Dominican mashed boiled plantain dish). Blenders and food processors are preferred to make *sofrito* but they cannot substitute for the *pilón* to make *mofongo* and *mangú* because these dishes get the shape of the mortar and are often served in it. A grater is indispensable in Caribbean cooking to prepare plantains, green bananas, and root vegetables for *pasteles* and other dishes. Food processors achieve the same results effortlessly, although many people prefer to use a hand grater for small quantities of food to avoid the hassle of assembling and cleaning the machine.

Pilón y maceta. © J. Susan Cole Stone.

Other tools used in the preparation of ingredients before cooking are electric mixers, sharp knives, mallets, and sieves. Electric mixers are useful for making the occasional cake, but they are indispensable to whip up the dough for tamales, incorporating enough air to make them spongy and tender. Knives are a must in all kitchens and a very sharp one is needed to slice fish for *ceviches*. Metal or wooden mallets are used to flatten and tenderize meats, and sieves are used to make smooth sauces and to strain coconut milk made by grinding fresh coconut with water in a blender.

The equipment used to cook is the same commonly found in kitchens in the United States: gas or electric stove plus microwave and toaster ovens. Specialized pots include earthenware *ollas* and *cazuelas* used by Mexican cooks. *Ollas* are pots used to cook beans, soups, and stews, while *cazuelas* are shaped like bowls with flat bottoms and are used for *moles*. Mexican earthenware is glazed inside and it is used directly over the flame or over a diffuser on electric burners. They retain heat uniformly and many argue that earthenware contributes to the taste of the food. Many people prefer not to use these pots because their glaze often contains lead and have switched to enameled cast iron because it has similar heat retention ability. Cooks that use Mexican earthenware are careful to avoid cooking acidic foods or storing food in them to prevent lead from leaching into the food.

Puerto Rican cooking needs a *caldero*, a heavy cast aluminum pot that is considered indispensable to cook rice, to deep fry, and to cook in general. Pressure cookers are very popular, particularly to accelerate the cooking of beans and stews that normally need long simmering times. A large steamer or *tamalera* available in Latino markets is ideal to cook tamales, although many people improvise one by placing a colander inside a large stock pot. Clay,

Olla. © J. Susan Cole Stone.

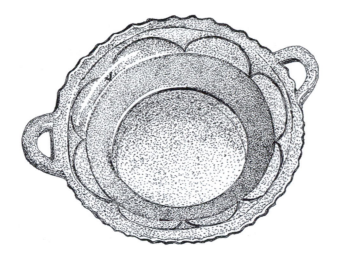

Cazuela. © J. Susan Cole Stone.

steel, or cast iron griddles (called *comal* in México and Central America, and *budare* in South America) are essential to cook tortillas, *pupusas*, and *arepas* (maize griddle cakes). They are also used by Mexican cooks to roast chiles and other ingredients.

Coffee is made in a stovetop espresso machine and consumed strong and black or with milk and sugar. There is also a method of preparing strong coffee by placing large amounts of ground coffee in boiling water and straining

Caldero. © J. Susan Cole Stone.

Cooking *pupusas* on a griddle. Courtesy of Douglas Gómez.

it with a cloth colander. Mexicans for special occasions make *café de olla*, coffee in an earthenware pot sweetened with dark sugar and flavored with cinnamon and other spices. Argentineans and other South American La-tinos drink *yerba mate*, a caffeinated infusion of *mate* leaves. The infusion is traditionally served in a gourd (which is also called *mate*) and drunk with a *bombilla*, a straw that strains the leaves as *mate* is drunk. *Yerba mate* is also more simply made using tea bag–style products.

Molcajete y tejolote. © J. Susan Cole Stone.

Mate y bombilla. © J. Susan Cole Stone.

There are many specialty tools that perform a single task. One of the most common is the tortilla press. Two hinged, flat disks made of wood or light cast iron are used to press a small ball of *masa* into a perfectly round and thin tortilla. They simplify the rolling and patting of tortillas, although it is necessary to line the base with plastic wrap to prevent tortillas from sticking. A similar instrument is a *tostonera*, which is a wooden press used to flatten plantains to make *tostones*. These come in two versions: the classic model that makes

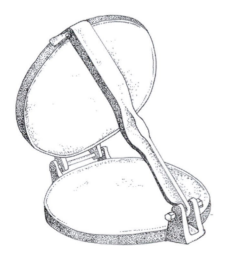

Tortilla press. © J. Susan Cole Stone.

Tostonera. © J. Susan Cole Stone.

flat *tostones*, and a fancier one that gives them a bowl shape to make stuffed *tostones*. Another instrument used to prepare plantains is a *mariquita* slicer. This is a simple wooden mandoline used to slice plantains very finely for fried plantain chips.

Molinillos are wooden stirrers used to whisk and froth chocolate and maize drinks like *atole*. They consist of ornately carved movable rings at the base of a handle. To froth a drink, the handle is rotated back and forth between the palms of both hands. A bean masher or a regular potato masher aids in the making of refried beans. A citrus reamer comes in handy given that Latino cooking uses plenty of citrus juices. Flan can be made in any baking pan inside a bigger one that holds some water but there are specialized pots for them called *flaneras*. These are double boiler pots with a flan mold insert that holds the custard over simmering water.

Electric appliances are available on the market to cook tortillas and *arepas* but they are not widely used because their performance is considered unsatisfactory. Electric tortilla makers are like a tortilla press but they cook the tortilla as they flatten the dough. *Arepa* makers are also like a press but they have round indentations both at the top and the bottom in which the dough is baked and shaped like fat griddle cakes. Electric rice cookers are quite common except among those who enjoy eating the crispy rice crust that forms at the bottom of a *caldero*. Sandwich presses are considered essential in cafeterias to make Cuban-style sandwiches. Restaurant cooks and street food vendors use specialized tools like spiral orange peelers, cane juice extractors, and citrus juicers. Another specialized kitchen gadget is a *churrera*, which is a plastic or metal syringe used to make the fried pastry called *churros*. Long, grooved strips of pastry dough are extruded from the *churrera* directly into hot oil.

Local Latino entrepreneurs have devised machines to help in the cooking of traditional foods in the U.S. context. Puerto Ricans in New York created a machine to make *pasteles*. The dough for *pasteles* is ideally made by finely grating green bananas, plantains, yuca, and other vegetables. The machine is built like a large food processor that grinds large quantities of vegetables in less time and with considerably less labor than using a hand grater. Another gadget available is a disk insert for food processors that grates the vegetables as finely as a hand grater. The machine has been embraced by those who make *pasteles* in very large batches for sale, but most home cooks are happy to use a regular food processor while others insist that only grating by hand produces a good result.

Cubans in Miami have created a machine to easily roast a whole pig without having to dig a pit or constantly turn it over a fire. The roasting box, also known as the Chinese box (*la caja china*), was inspired by a Chinese technique. It consists of a wooden box lined with aluminum in which a whole butterflied pig encased in a grid can be roasted in as little as four hours. The top of the box is covered with charcoal and the pig cooks in the closed box until it is time to turn it around to place the skin side up to make it crisp and golden. This box has been embraced by barbecue connoisseurs all over the United States.

NOTES

1. Sarah J. Mahler, *Salvadorans in Suburbia: Symbiosis and Conflict* (Boston: Allyn and Bacon, 1995), p. 86.

2. Katherine Cason et al., "Dietary Intake and Food Security among Migrant Farm Workers in Pennsylvania," *Harris School Working Paper Series* 4, no. 2, November 2003.

3. Daniel Melero Malpica, "Indigenous Mexican Migrants in a Modern Metropolis: The Reconstruction of Latino Communities in Los Angeles," in *Latino Los Angeles: Transformations, Communities, and Activism*, ed. Enrique C. Ochoa and Gilda L. Ochoa (Tucson: University of Arizona Press, 2005), p. 121.

4. Daniel D. Arreola, *Tejano South Texas: A Mexican American Cultural Province* (Austin: University of Texas Press, 2002), p. 167.

5. Zilkia Janer, "(In)Edible Nature: New World Food and Coloniality," *Cultural Studies* 21, nos. 2–3 (March/May 2007): 402–403.

4

Meals

Latino food is generally based on maize, beans, rice, plantains, yuca, squashes, and capsicum peppers. This does not mean that all Latinos eat the same food since different culinary traditions use the same ingredients in different ways, with different techniques, emphasis, and combinations. The result is a kaleidoscopic cuisine in which foods might seem the same but are actually significantly different. In the United States, the proximity between Latinos from different countries has made it possible for Latinos to see the similarities and differences between their food cultures. The similarities become even stronger because all the cuisines are subject to the same constraints in the United States. They all lack the full variety of local ingredients and seasonings that give each cuisine its own character and depend on the same reduced pool of ingredients from the supermarket or even from the *mercados* (markets) that sell many but by no means all the necessary ingredients. Another factor that brings Latino culinary cultures closer together is the need to adapt to the way in which time is managed in the United States in which significantly less time is available for cooking and eating. However, Latinos resist homogenization and insist on keeping the distinctiveness of their culinary cultures alive. While many Latinos come from urban middle-class backgrounds in Latin America where eating patterns already conform to European and Anglo American ones, other Latinos come from peasant and indigenous backgrounds and try to maintain their food habits as much as possible.

The struggle to assert Latino national identities is not new. Latin American countries since independence have strived to establish national identities capable of representing multiethnic nations. Most Latin American countries have officially or unofficially designated one or more dishes as *plato nacional*, a dish that is supposed to represent national culinary culture. The dishes are chosen either because they use local ingredients, because they combine foods from different regions and ethnic groups of the country, or because they are the indispensable daily food of the majority of the population. In some cases more than one country has claimed the same dish as their national dish. Both Perú and Ecuador claim *ceviche* (raw citrus-marinated pieces of fish and seafood) as their national dish, while hearty stews that combine different meats, plantains, and root vegetables called *ajiaco* in Cuba and *sancocho* in the Dominican Republic, Colombia, Panamá, and other countries are considered national by them all. *Sancocho*, a coherent whole composed of many disparate parts, is supposed to represent the multiethnic nations. The fact that the same dish is considered a national dish in more than one country puts into question their uniqueness, making obvious that cuisine does not respect national borders. Latin American cuisines have much in common with each other, particularly inside the same region. Many countries like México and Colombia have significant regional differences, making it impossible to choose a single national dish to represent their cuisine as a whole. The selection of national dishes is related to the need of nation states to establish a coherent and distinctive national identity, and both national identity and national cuisines are contested constructs that can evoke powerful emotions.

Many *platos nacionales* are taken from peasant cooking, and urban residents in Latin America might eat them only sporadically if at all. However, in the U.S. context such dishes are reclaimed and are proudly served at home and at restaurants as an identity affirmation ritual. Latinos can have heated arguments regarding the proper execution of a national dish, claiming that their own local or even personal way of preparing the dish is the best and most legitimate. In the United States, where the incredibly diverse populations of Latin American origin are racialized and grouped together under the rubric of *Latino* or *Hispanic*, the ideal of national cultures and cuisines is revived in an attempt to resist a homogenization that for many Latinos implies a loss of status. The emergence of pan-Latino cuisine rearticulates Latin American national and regional differences in the U.S. context, rather than erases them.

Latino meals are not always meals that would be considered "typical" in their countries of origin. Latinos are as likely to experiment with and adapt to new foods as anybody else. Still, frequently they have meals that to the extent possible reproduce the traditional meals they or their family grew up with. What constitutes a meal and how they are spread throughout the day varies as much as the names that are used to refer to them. Breakfast, generally called *desayuno*, is the first meal of the day and it can be light or quite heavy, depending on the time when the next meal is expected. *Almuerzo* (lunch) can mean a regular mid-day lunch or, in the case of Mexican

Americans, a mid-morning meal that follows a very light *desayuno*. A heavier and later lunch is called *comida* among Latinos that will have only a light supper in the evening called *cena*, while for those that have a moderate mid-day *almuerzo*, *comida* refers to their heavier evening meal. Breakfast and lunch are the meals most affected by life in the United States because of the demands of work schedules that do not allow for leisurely meal breaks in the middle of the day. Many Latinos have switched to cold cereal and other convenient Anglo American–style breakfasts, and have only sandwiches, salads, and fast foods at lunch time. Latino breakfasts can be very small or very large. Small breakfasts can be nothing more than coffee and bread, while large breakfasts cannot be distinguished from lunch or dinner because they include the same kinds of dishes like rice, beans, and meat. Many Latinos do not have traditional breakfasts often but cherish having them on weekends or on special occasions. With some exceptions, coffee is the premier breakfast drink. Traditional drinks that are served with meals in Latin America are gradually being replaced by carbonated beverages. Dinner is the meal that is more likely to adhere to traditional eating patterns because people have more time to prepare it after coming home from work and it is generally consumed relatively late in the evening. While rice and beans or tortillas and beans are the base of most traditional Latino meals, there is an incredible variety of ways to prepare them and a vast number of main and side dishes to go with them.

MEXICAN AMERICANS

Because the Mexican American population is so large and its history is so long, Mexican American food has developed at least two different but complementary sides. On the one hand there are Mexican American eating patterns that remain close to regional Mexican ones because strong Mexican communities nourished by constant immigration keep them alive. On the other hand there are culinary practices that distinguish Mexican American food from Mexican food and that were shaped by the impact of a long period without appropriate ingredients and facing the demand to cater and adapt to Anglo American taste. Both sides have a space and sometimes come together at the table in Mexican American homes. Mexican American home meals are different from what are seen in restaurants. Most restaurants serve what Mexicans call *antojitos*, which are considered street food or snacks and appetizers. Restaurants also serve fancy dishes like the very complex *moles* (meat or chicken in sauces made with ground nuts, chiles, and spices), which are cooked at home only for special occasions. Mexican home meals include but are not limited to the snacks and festive dishes that are usually served in restaurants.

A light Mexican American breakfast includes coffee or chocolate, fruit juice, and *pan dulce* or *bolillos*. *Pan dulce* is a sweet egg-enriched bread roll and *bolillos* are crusty rolls used to make *tortas* (sandwiches). A common breakfast treat is *molletes*, a hollowed *bolillo* stuffed with refried beans. A classic breakfast combination, *churros con chocolate*, consists of deep fried pastry strips served with a cup of thick cinnamon-flavored Mexican chocolate. *Chilaquiles* are a very popular dish made by simmering fried maize tortilla pieces in spicy salsa. The top is sprinkled with cheese and they are sometimes served with eggs, meat, or chicken. Egg dishes are common in Mexican breakfasts. They include *huevos rancheros*, a dish of fried eggs served on fried tortillas with a ranch-style salsa made with roasted tomatoes, garlic, and *serrano* chiles. Another egg dish, called *huevos motuleños*, comes from the Yucatán region. In this preparation eggs are served on lightly fried tortillas that have been spread with refried beans. The dish is covered with salsa and garnished with cheese, peas, and ham. *Huevos a la mexicana* are scrambled eggs, chiles, onion, and tomatoes garnished with fresh cheese and avocado. Soups can also be served for breakfast. Two favorite ones are fresh fish and seafood soups flavored with chile, and the spicy tripe soup *menudo*, regarded as a cure for hangovers.

Mexican American lunches and dinners at home are built around a main dish of chicken, beef, pork, fish, or shellfish. Chicken can be stewed or cooked in different sauces and special preparations like *pipián*, a sauce made with ground pumpkin seeds and chiles. Common beef dishes include *carne con chile colorado* (beef in red chile sauce), *albóndigas en chipotle* (chipotle-flavored meatballs), and *pasta mexicana* (ground beef with hot salsa served over spaghetti). Pork is served often as *chile verde con puerco y papas* (pork and potatoes in green chile sauce) and *cochinita pibil* style (seasoned with orange juice and annatto paste and cooked in the oven instead of in a pit). Fish is served in a variety of sauces, and shrimp are served in seafood cocktails or seasoned with chipotle when prepared *a la diabla*.

Enchiladas of all kinds are frequent main dishes or light meals. Enchiladas are maize tortillas that are briefly fried in oil and dipped in spicy salsa before being folded or rolled around a filling of cheese, vegetables, fish, or any kind of meat. The filled enchiladas are served on a platter garnished with more salsa and a little grated *queso añejo* (aged cheese). Rice and refried beans are always served at table as side dishes. Other common side dishes include potatoes, green beans, maize, and stuffed vegetables like *chayote* squash, zucchini, and sweet potatoes. *Sopa seca* made with rice or with vermicelli noodles can be served as a light meal or as a separate course of a large meal. Although *sopa seca* literally means "dry soup," it is not a soup but a dish in which rice or noodles are cooked in a well-seasoned broth with tomatoes, onion, and garlic until the broth is absorbed.

Salads are important components of Mexican American meals. Among the most common ones there are *nopal* (cactus paddle) salad, potato salads, green salads, and salads that feature jícama, orange, and melon. In contrast to Mexican salads, Mexican American salads use ingredients like lettuce and broccoli more frequently than *verdolagas* (purslane) and *quelites* (lamb's quarters), which are not easily available in the United States. Soups are another important part of Mexican and Mexican American meals. There are vegetable cream soups made with avocado, carrot, or *chayote* squash, as well as black bean soup, red snapper soup, and meatball soup. Heavier soups like *pozole* (hominy stew) and *menudo* can be meals in themselves. Different salsas and *encurtidos* (pickled vegetables like onions and carrots) are provided with meals so each person can use them according to his or her taste. Drinks that are served with meals include *aguas frescas* (fresh fruit drinks), *horchata* (rice drink), and *atole* (maize drinks). Desserts might be flan (caramel custard), ice cream, rice pudding, or gelatins flavored with fruit, *rompope* (eggnog), or coffee liqueur.

Albóndigas en Chipotle (Mexican Meatballs in Chipotle Chile Sauce)

For the sauce:

1 1/2 pound tomatoes, chopped
2 cloves garlic, chopped

2 canned *chipotle* chiles in *adobo* sauce
1 cup water
1 TBSP olive oil

For the meatballs:

1 pound ground beef
1/2 pound ground pork
1 clove garlic, minced
2 eggs

1/2 tsp Mexican dried oregano
1/2 tsp cumin
1/4 tsp ground black pepper
1 tsp salt

Puree the tomatoes, garlic, and chiles in a blender or food processor. Stir in the water. Heat the oil over medium high heat in a large pot or Dutch oven. Cook the sauce in the hot oil for 5 minutes. Lower the heat and simmer the sauce for 5 more minutes. Mix all the meatball ingredients thoroughly in a bowl. Shape the meat mixture into balls of any size desired. Drop the meatballs into the simmering sauce for about 30 minutes or until cooked. Stir occasionally and add more water to the sauce if necessary during the cooking process.

CARIBBEAN AMERICANS

Caribbean American meals are based on rice and beans with a meat, poultry, or seafood main dish and a variety of side dishes. Caribbean cuisine in general is mildly spiced and rarely uses hot chiles. Most dishes are flavored with *sofrito*, a combination of ground onions, garlic, bell peppers, *ajíes dulces* (sweet chiles), cilantro, *recao* (long leaf cilantro), and other ingredients that can vary from person to person. Additional ingredients might be olives, capers, ham, oregano, and lime juice, among many others. *Sofrito* is briefly sautéed in *achiote* (annatto) colored and flavored lard or oil before the addition of tomatoes or broth to make all kinds of rice and bean dishes, soups, and stews. The most important drink is coffee, followed by tropical fruit juices and milkshakes called *batidos*. Caribbean meals end with a cup of coffee and maybe a little dessert. Many desserts like flan come from the Spanish tradition while others are Caribbean creations using cane sugar to transform coconut, guavas, papaya, and milk into a wide variety of sweets. Caribbean American meals in general remain very similar to traditional Caribbean ones.

Cuban Americans

Cuban Americans have kept their cuisine close to what it was like in Cuba before the Cuban Revolution. However, contemporary Cuban and Cuban American cuisines have become dissimilar since the former has evolved in a context of food shortages while the latter has developed in the midst of abundance. A Cuban American breakfast can be as simple as *pan cubano* (lard-enriched bread with a crisp crust and an airy interior) and *café cubano* (strong espresso with sugar). For lunch and dinner Cuban Americans stew black beans and serve them with white rice, or cook them with rice to make *moros y cristianos*. Black beans are also baked and used as the main ingredient in soups and salads. Rice dishes include *paella*, Chinese fried rice, and rice cooked with red beans, chicken, or calamari. Frequent side dishes are fried green or ripe plantains, *boniato* (Latin American sweet potato), and yuca.

Pork is generally fried in chunks or marinated in garlic and citrus *mojo* and roasted. Roast pork slices are used to make the classic sandwiches *pan con lechón* and *cubano*. *Pan con lechón* is made with Cuban bread and roasted pork dressed with butter and onions, while the *cubano* sandwich is more elaborate. It is made with Cuban bread spread with butter and yellow mustard, and filled with layers of roasted pork, ham, Swiss cheese, and dill pickles. The same fillings and flavorings inside a yellow and sweet long bun is called a *medianoche* or "midnight" sandwich. Other pork dishes include grilled pork in garlic sauce, *chorizo* sausage, and ham and potato croquettes, as well as grilled and braised dishes. Pork is sometimes cooked with sauces flavored with fruits like mango, papaya, and bitter orange.

Cuban Americans prepare beef in steaks and in popular preparations like *picadillo, ropa vieja, rabo encendido,* and *boliche. Picadillo* is ground beef cooked with tomatoes, bell peppers, onion, and garlic and flavored with black pepper, cumin, and cayenne pepper. It is served as a main dish with white rice, fried plantains, and maybe fried eggs, or it is used as a stuffing for vegetables and for turnovers called *empanadillas. Ropa vieja,* which literally means "old clothes," is flank steak that is poached with seasoning vegetables and then shredded and cooked in a tomato sauce with onions and peppers. The dish got its name because the tender long shreds of meat resemble a pile of well-worn rags. *Rabo encendido* is an oxtail stew, and *boliche* is a pot roast that might include potatoes or chorizo. Cuban Americans also make their own meatloaf version called *pulpeta.* Chicken is baked, stewed, and roasted, or it can be prepared in tomato- or garlic-based sauces. Fish is fried or cooked in tomato-based sauces, and conch salad and *bacalao* dishes are also common. Cuban Americans add rum to enhance the flavor of many dishes, from stews and sauces to glazes that are sometimes flavored with papaya, guava, or bitter orange.

Soups that round up a traditional Cuban meal include black bean soup, Galician stew, and shrimp, corn, and potato soup. The thick vegetable stew called *ajiaco* could be a meal by itself but it is usually served with rice and beans. *Ajiaco* combines green plantains, maize, *calabaza,* and root vegetables like yuca, malanga, *boniato,* and *ñame* with meats like beef, pork, chicken, and *chorizo* to form a hearty stew. Other meal accompaniments are salads like avocado and onion salad, and a wide variety of fritters and croquettes. The dessert options are quite extensive and they include flan, tropical fruit ice creams, and puddings. Rum is frequently used to flavor cakes, puddings, and dessert sauces. A well-known Cuban bread pudding called *diplomático* is made with dry Cuban bread baked with milk, eggs, butter, sugar, almonds, and raisins.

Ropa Vieja (Cuban Shredded Beef)

1 1/2 pound flank steak	1 TBSP olive oil
2 onions, one chopped and one halved	1 green Italian frying or bell pepper, chopped
4 cloves garlic, two whole and two minced	1–2 serrano chiles, chopped
1 carrot	3 tomatoes, chopped
1 rib celery	1 1/2 cup reserved broth
1 bay leaf	Salt and pepper to taste

(continued)

Put the steak, halved onion, whole garlic, carrot, celery, and bay leaf in a large pot with enough water to cover and bring to a boil. Reduce the heat and simmer, covered, for 1 1/2 hours. Let the meat cool in the liquid, then drain and reserve the broth. Finely shred the meat by hand in a bowl. In a large skillet heat the oil on medium heat and sauté the chopped onion, pepper, and garlic for 5 minutes or until soft. Add chiles, tomatoes, and broth and simmer uncovered for 15 minutes or until thickened. Mix in the shredded beef and season with salt and pepper. Cook for 15 more minutes and serve.

Dominican Americans

Dominican Americans have continued their traditional dietary habits in the United States. The distinctively Dominican dish called *mangú* is an important part of Dominican American meals and it is eaten at any meal, including breakfast. For this dish, boiled green plantains are mashed with oil or butter and served with a topping of sautéed onions. At breakfast time *mangú* is accompanied by fried white cheese, *salchichón* sausage, or fried eggs. Oatmeal, omelettes, and bread are other frequent breakfast foods.

The standard daily lunch or dinner of rice, beans, and meat is called *bandera* (flag) because it is supposed to represent national culture like a flag.

Dominican breakfast. Clockwise from top left: fried cheese, *mangú*, pickled onions, longaniza sausage, and fried eggs. Photo by Zilkia Janer.

Dominicans combine rice with beans and meat in the same way as Puerto Ricans and Cubans and also in less usual combinations. Rice cooked with beans is called *moro* and it can be made with red, black, or fava beans, or with pigeon peas and coconut. Rice dishes with meat are called *locrio* and traditional combinations include *locrio* of shrimp, *bacalao*, *chorizo*, *longaniza* sausage, chicken, spicy canned sardines, or *arenques* (smoked herrings). Other rice dishes are *chofán* (Dominican Chinese fried rice), rice with noodles, rice with maize, and rice with hearts of palm.

Roast pork and stewed chicken and beef seasoned with *sofrito* are common preparations. *Mondongo, sancocho*, oxtail stew, and stews made with goat, herring, or conch are other dishes favored by Dominican Americans. *Chicharrón de pollo*, crispy pieces of fried chicken seasoned with black pepper and oregano, is another popular dish. Fish is cooked in coconut milk or fried and served with a butter, lemon, parsley, and black pepper sauce. Dominicans prepare many different kinds of layered casseroles called *pastelones* that are made with ripe plantain, eggplant, yuca, cornmeal, or potatoes with a beef, pork, or chicken filling. Casseroles are also made with spaghetti and other kinds of pasta. Appetizers and side dishes include pan-Latino dishes like fried green and ripe plantains, *empanaditas* (turnovers), and croquettes. Many Dominican fritters are made with yuca, like cheese-stuffed yuca balls and *cativías* (yuca turnovers). *Quipe*, a favorite fritter, comes from the Middle East and it is a bulgur wheat patty stuffed with meat.

Dominican desserts include pan-Latino favorites like flan, puddings, and tropical fruit–based sweets. *Dulce de coco* (coconut fudge), dulce de leche (caramelized milk), and *majarete* (cornmeal pudding) are also common. Puddings are made with bread, sweet potato, or rice. A cherished Dominican dessert is *habichuelas con dulce*, made with pureed red kidney beans boiled with milk, coconut milk, cubed sweet potatoes, raisins, and sugar, and spiced with cinnamon, cloves, and nutmeg. This sweetened bean cream is served hot or chilled, sometimes with a few cookies floating on top. This dessert was originally prepared only for Easter but now it is enjoyed year-round.

Puerto Ricans in the United States

The dietary habits of Puerto Ricans living on the island and Puerto Ricans living in the United States are almost identical. Circular migration and the close relationship between Puerto Rico and the United States has kept Puerto Rican cuisine developing along the same lines in both places. A Puerto Rican breakfast can be just coffee with either toasts or *criollo* bread (similar to French bread), and scrambled or fried eggs. Many Puerto Ricans also like hot cereals like oatmeal, farina, and cornmeal mush, or a quick custard made with cornstarch. For lunch or dinner rice can be white and served with stewed beans, or it can be cooked with beans or with chicken, codfish, sausages, or crab meat. Puerto Ricans eat a wide variety of beans and peas, and there are some classic ways of cooking them like rice with pigeon peas, white beans with *calabaza* squash, pigeon peas with *bolitas de plátano* (grated green plantain dumplings), and chickpeas with salted pork hocks.

Pork is a clear favorite and it is always present in one way or another. Lard rendered from fatback pieces and colored with annatto is the ideal fat used to sauté the basic *sofrito*. Ham bones and salted pork hocks are used to flavor beans, stews, and rice. Pork chops are fried or stewed, and cubed pork is fried with garlic and onions and served with *tostones* (twice-fried green plantain slices) or *mofongo* (ground fried green plantains flavored with garlic and bits of *chicharrón* [pork rind]). Specialty dishes made with pork's innards are *gandinga* (stewed pork's heart, kidney, and liver) and *mondongo* (pork tripe and chickpea stew).

Puerto Ricans serve chicken fried, stewed, or oven roasted with a stuffing of mashed fried green plantains, yuca, or yautía. Beef is preferred in stews or in thin steaks that are breaded and fried (*bistec empanado*) or cooked in vinegar and olive oil with plenty of onions (*bistec encebollado*). Canned corned beef, Vienna sausages, and other processed meats are stewed in tomato sauce with *sofrito* to make quick and economical meals. Seafood like octopus, conch, and crab is prepared in cold salads with vinegar, olive oil, onions, garlic, and pimento-stuffed olives. These salads are often used to stuff *tostones* and *mofongo*. Fish is fried and served with a tomato sauce called *mojito isleño*, not to be confused with the Cuban rum, lime, and mint cocktail also called *mojito*. The tomato sauce is simmered with onions, garlic, vinegar, olives, capers, and bay leaves and it is also used as a dipping sauce for *tostones* and other fried foods. Main dish soups called *asopao* are thick with rice and plenty of shrimp or chicken. Dry salted codfish or *bacalao* is the base of many traditional dishes. It can be simply boiled with plantains, green bananas, and root vegetables, and dressed with olive oil and onions to make a *serenata*, or it can be stewed or cooked with scrambled eggs or with rice.

The basic Puerto Rican salad is made with lettuce and tomato dressed with vinaigrette, and avocado, onion, and canned vegetables like corn, carrots, and peas are frequently added. Potato salads and baked potatoes are popular side dishes. Vegetables like eggplants, bell peppers, tomatoes, onions, and *chayote* squash are often stuffed with ground meat. Main dish vegetable dishes include *pastelón*, which is a layered casserole made with stewed ground meat and mashed potatoes or ripe plantain slices.

Traditional desserts are coconut, *calabaza*, cheese or caramel flan, *arroz con dulce* (thick coconut milk rice pudding), *tembleque* (coconut milk custard), and *dulce de lechosa* (papaya slices in a cinnamon-flavored syrup). Sweet guava paste served with salty fresh cheese *queso del país* is a classic dessert combination enjoyed by Puerto Ricans and many other Latinos.

Mofongo (Puerto Rican Mashed Fried Plantains)

3 green plantains
4 cloves garlic
1/4 pound *chicharrón* (pork
  cracklings) or 6 slices
  cooked bacon

1/2 tsp salt
Oil for frying

Peel the plantains and slice them 1/2 inch thick. Fry the plantain slices in hot oil until cooked but not crispy. In a mortar and pestle mash the garlic with a little salt. Add the fried plantain slices and *chicharrón* and pound until mashed, making sure all the seasonings are evenly distributed. Form into balls and serve as a side dish with meat, chicken, or seafood.

CENTRAL AMERICANS IN THE UNITED STATES

The meals of Central Americans in the United States, as well as in Central America, are generally based on beans, maize in the form of tortillas and tamales, rice, plantains, squash, avocado, and eggs. Latinos from northern Central America (Salvadorans, Guatemalans, and Hondurans) share a Maya culinary cultural framework with southern México, whereas Latinos from southern Central America (Nicaraguans, Costa Rican, and Panamanians) have stronger influences from Europe, Asia, Africa, and the United States. Salvadoran, Guatemalan, and Honduran American meals are characterized by the use of tortillas and beans in most meals, while rice and beans have the central role in Nicaraguan, Costa Rican, and Panamanian American meals. Central American tortillas are fatter than Mexican tortillas, which allows for them to be split opened and stuffed. While many of the words used for Central American foods are the same Mexican words that are widely used in the United States, the foods that they designate in different countries often vary slightly and sometimes dramatically. Quesadillas, for example, are tortillas with cheese in Mexican cuisine but in Salvadoran cuisine they are sweet cheesecakes. Central Americans in the United States consume a wide variety of drinks with and between meals, including coffee, fresh fruit drinks called *frescos, chichas* (fermented drinks made of maize or fruits), chocolate drinks, oatmeal drinks, *horchata,* and *atoles.* Industrial versions of these drinks are imported and easily available in the United States. The desserts traditionally preferred by Central Americans are rice pudding, sweet tamales, and banana, yuca, or fresh cheese–based sweets. Central Americans in the United States are able to continue their national and regional food cultures to a great extent.

Costa Ricans in the United States

A Costa Rican breakfast can be French bread with sour cream or with butter and jam, or rice and beans cooked together in the traditional dish called *gallo pinto* that is the base of many meals. Costa Rican *gallo pinto* is made with black beans and seasoned with bell peppers, onion, and garlic. *Gallo pinto* and many other dishes are seasoned with the incredibly popular Lizano brand sauce. A basic meal is composed of rice and beans with side dishes like fried ripe plantain, cabbage and tomato salad, eggs, potato salad, and spaghetti. Rice dishes other than *gallo pinto* include fried rice, soupy *arroz guacho,* and rice with chicken, shrimp, maize, or hearts of palm. Another side dish is called *barbudos* (literally "bearded"), which are green bean omelettes in which the long green beans look like the strands of a beard.

Costa Ricans make many different kinds of *picadillo,* which is a dish of diced or minced vegetables cooked with tomato, garlic, onions, and peppers and that may or may not include meat. If meat is used, the most frequent one is pork but any meat and canned tuna are also options. Vegetables frequently cooked in *picadillo* are potatoes, *chayote* squash with fresh maize, green papaya, green beans with carrots, green plantain, and zucchini. Oftentimes *picadillos* are eaten inside a tortilla in the form of *gallos* (tacos).

Costa Rican tamales include *tamales de elote* (fresh maize tamales), bean tamales, and more elaborate pork or chicken tamales. A favorite Costa Rican ingredient is the peach palm fruit called *pejibaye,* which they use in tamales, *picadillos,* and crackers. There are also many plantain-based dishes, from green plantain soup and plantain fritters to plantain empanadas (turnovers). Ripe plantain empanadas have a mashed bean or grated cheese filling, and green plantain empanadas have chicken and other savory fillings. During meals Costa Ricans enjoy fresh fruit drinks called *frescos* and for dessert they might have rice pudding, fried bananas flambé, and fruits in syrup.

Guatemalan Americans

A complete Guatemalan American breakfast includes fried or scrambled eggs, sometimes dressed with a red chile and tomato salsa called *chirmol, frijoles volteados* (similar to refried beans but cooked until they form a thick mass), tortillas or bread rolls, fresh cheese, and fried ripe plantains. Lunch and dinner can also be as simple as beans, tortillas, and eggs. Meals always include tortillas and different kinds of *chirmoles*. More elaborate main dishes include meats cooked in *moles* (sauces made with ground chiles, nuts, and spices) and in *pepián* (sauce made with ground chiles, sesame, and pumpkin seeds). Herbs like bay leaves, thyme, and basil are frequently used and many dishes make use of *miltomates* (green husk tomatoes or *tomatillos*). For the classic dish *carne en miltomate*, pork is cooked in a sauce of *miltomates* and onions. Another classic dish is *pollo en crema con loroco*, in which a chicken is cooked in cream, green onions or leeks, garlic, and *loroco* flowers. Another Guatemalan favorite is layered casseroles called *tapados*. One of the most popular is *tapado de coco*, in which fried fish is layered with slices of yuca, green and ripe plantains, and covered with coconut milk and tomatoes that have been fried with garlic and onions. A stew of white beans and pork backbone or ribs is another popular dish.

For special occasions Guatemalans prepare a wide variety of tamales like *tamales rojos* filled with pork and a red sauce made with tomatoes, chiles, and annatto; black tamales made with meat and a dark sauce made with ground burnt bread rolls, chocolate, prunes, and ground sesame and pumpkin seeds; and the simpler *tamalitos* that have string beans, *loroco* flowers, and *chipilín* leaves mixed into the maize dough. Treats that are enjoyed more frequently are made with tortillas. A Guatemalan enchilada consists of a fried tortilla that is lined with a lettuce leaf that holds seasoned chopped meat topped with *chirmol* and *curtido* (pickled vegetables), and it is garnished with grated dry cheese and hard-boiled eggs. A tostada is a simpler dish in which a fried tortilla is topped with either refried beans, guacamole, or salsa and garnished with grated cheese and raw onion rings. Another common tortilla dish is *tortilla mixta*, which is the Guatemalan way of preparing hot dogs. A cooked hot dog is placed in a folded tortilla that is lined with guacamole and seasoned cabbage and topped to taste with onions, radishes, lime juice, mustard, or mayonnaise.

Vegetable side dishes include Guatemalan *guaque* chiles stuffed with meat, and *chilaquilas de güisquil*. To make the latter, a slice of fresh cheese is sandwiched between two slices of cooked *chayote* squash, dipped in an egg and flour batter, and fried. It is served with a tomato, onion, and chile sauce on top or on the side. Vegetables are also used in sweet preparations that can be served as dessert or as a snack. The most common are *rellenitos* (fried ovals of mashed ripe plantains stuffed with sweetened mashed black beans) and *chancletas de güisquil* (hollowed *chayote* squash skin halves stuffed with chayote pulp mixed with eggs, sugar, raisins, bread crumbs, and cinnamon). The ideal ending of a Guatemalan meal is a cup of coffee with a variety of sweet breads.

Honduran Americans

A traditional Honduran American breakfast has the same components as an evening meal. It comprises eggs, refried beans, tortillas, and grilled meat, with *chorizo* sausage or *chicharrón* (fried pork rind), fried ripe plantains, cheese, and avocado as frequent accompaniments. Honduran meals can feature soups like *mondongo* (tripe stew), meatball soup, *sopa de capirotadas* (maize dumpling soup), and crab soup. For the famous *sopa de caracol*, conch is cooked in coconut milk with butter, plantains, yuca, chiles, and cilantro. Conch is also prepared in *ceviche* or fried with eggs, onion, and chiles. Hondurans enjoy a great variety of *tapados* like the casserole-like *tapado seco*, in which meat and *chorizo* sausages are layered with green bananas, green and ripe plantains, potatoes, and fresh maize, and covered with coconut milk. Coconut milk is also used to make a flatbread called *pan de coco* and to cook rice and beans together in *casamiento*. Another common Honduran dish is *yuca con chicharrón*, a dish of boiled yuca dressed with cabbage salad, *chirmol*, and fried pork rind pieces. A specialty dish called *carne prensada* is a meatloaf spiced with cinnamon, cloves, and nutmeg that is steamed inside a cloth bag. It is served sliced with pickled vegetables (*curtido*).

The Honduran snack and light meal repertoire includes dishes with intriguing names like *baleadas*, *burras*, and *pastelitos de perro*. *Baleadas*, which literally means "shot with bullets," are folded wheat tortillas filled with mashed beans and *mantequilla crema* (Honduran sour cream). Beans are popularly known as *balas* (bullets), hence the name of this dish. *Burras*, literally "female donkeys," are a portable package made with maize tortillas, beans, scrambled eggs and mortadella, *chorizo* sausage or beef. *Pastelitos de perro*, which translates as "dog turnovers," are made with maize dough filled with ground beef and mashed potatoes that have been flavored and colored with annatto.

Nicaraguan Americans

The national dish of Nicaragua is red beans cooked with rice, onions, garlic, and bay leaves. It is called *gallo pinto*, which literally translates as "spotted rooster," because of the colorful effect that the beans give to the rice. *Gallo pinto* is the core of most traditional meals, including breakfast. Common side dishes include fried ripe plantains, cheese, eggs, meat, and salad. *Pinolillo*, a maize and cacao drink that Nicaraguans enjoy throughout the day, is traditionally served in a gourd.

Beef soup, red bean soup, and meatball soup are frequently served for lunch and dinner. A favorite snack or side dish is *vigorón*, a dish of yuca topped with *chicharrón* and a cabbage, tomato, and onion salad. Another traditional dish is *indio viejo*, which means "old Indian," presumably because it has a soft texture that is appropriate for people that cannot chew. *Indio viejo* consists of beef or chicken that has been boiled, shredded, and fried in a sauce that is further cooked in a thick broth made with maize *masa* (dough used to make tortillas). Nicaraguans frequently enjoy *churrasco con chimichurri*, the Argentinean-origin combination of grilled tenderloin steak with a parsley and garlic sauce. Nicaraguan varieties of tamales include the large *nacatamal* that has a filling inside as well as mixed into the maize dough; the sweet *yoltamal* made with fresh maize, milk, and fresh cheese; and the savory *montucas* made with fresh maize and a pork filling.

Two of the favorite desserts of Nicaraguans are *buñuelos* and *pastel tres leches*. *Buñuelos* are round fritters made with ground rice, yuca, and dry cheese. *Pastel tres leches* (three milk cake) is a cake that has been soaked in fresh milk, evaporated milk, and condensed milk and that is sometimes topped with meringue or whipped cream.

Gallo Pinto (Costa Rican/Nicaraguan Beans and Rice)

3 cups cooked white rice	1 small onion, chopped
2 cups cooked black or red beans, or 1 15-ounce can (drained)	3 cloves garlic, minced
	4 TBSP cilantro, roughly chopped
1 TBSP olive oil	1/2 tsp salt, or to taste
1 small green bell pepper, chopped	1 TBSP Worcestershire or Lizano sauce, optional

Heat the oil in a pot over medium heat and sauté the pepper, onion, and garlic 5–10 minutes until soft. Add the beans, rice, and cilantro, combining everything well and cook until heated through. Season with salt and sauce to taste. Serve with eggs, white cheese, and fried ripe plantains.

Panamanian Americans

A Panamanian American breakfast can be as simple as bread, eggs, fruits, and juice, or it can include fritters like *hojaldras* (doughnuts) and *carimañolas* (ground yuca fritters stuffed with eggs and meat). It can also be Panamanian tortillas, which are thick griddle cakes made with fresh maize with or without fresh cheese. The basic lunch and dinner consists of white rice, beans, and meat. Panamanian Americans prepare a wide variety of dishes that they have in common with other Latinos like tamales, *ceviches, mondongo* (tripe stew), *gallo pinto* (rice cooked with beans), *ropa vieja* (shredded beef), *tajadas* (fried ripe plantain slices), and *patacones* (fried green plantain slices). Popular rice dishes are rice with vegetables, crab, or chicken, and coconut rice with pigeon peas (*arroz con guandu y coco*) or with salted codfish (*arroz con bacalao y coco*). Yuca is enjoyed fried as a side dish, in salads and casseroles, and in a grated yuca, coconut, and cheese cake called *enyucado*. Soups include plantain soup made with plantains that have been fried and ground, thick rice stews made with seafood (*guacho de mariscos*) or with pigeon peas (*guacho de guandu*), and *sancocho*, the thick stew that is considered the national dish. Panamanian *sancocho* is made with chicken and *ñame* (yam) and its main seasoning is *culantro* (long leaf cilantro). This hearty stew can also contain plantains, yuca, and maize, and it is usually served with rice.

Panamanian culinary culture is also significantly influenced by West Indians that have brought Afro Antillean, Indian, and Chinese dishes. *Souse*, an appetizer of pork hocks marinated in lime and chiles, is one of the many West Indian dishes that have been adopted by Panamanians. There is also *fufu*, a soup made with coconut milk, fish, plantain, yuca, and *ñames*. Because of the Canal Zone, the influence of the United States in Panamanian cooking is also significant, as exemplified by the popularity of the ground meat, noodles, and cheese casserole called Johnny Mazetti.

Salvadoran Americans

A Salvadoran American breakfast is based on beans that can be refried, stewed, or in *casamiento* (cooked with rice, green chile, and garlic). Beans can be accompanied with tortillas or bread, cheese, *crema salvadoreña* (Salvadoran sour cream), fried or baked ripe plantains, and eggs. *Pupusas*, considered the national dish, can also be served for breakfast. *Pupusas* are fat tortillas stuffed with cheese, beans, and/or pork rind, served with *curtido*, a combination of pickled vegetables like cabbage, onion, and carrots. Salvadorans can also have just *pan dulce* for breakfast or eggs with *chorizo* sausage.

A basic Salvadoran American lunch or dinner consists of refried black or red beans or stewed black, red, or white beans with rice or tortillas and some meat. Chicken, beef, and pork can be fried, stewed, or roasted. Special preparations include *chanfaina* (beef or pork liver mixed with corn) and *gallo en chicha*. While the former is a homey dish, the latter is a festive dish in which a rooster is cooked in fermented pineapple juice, onions, and tomatoes with sweet seasonings like unrefined sugar, raisins, and prunes. There are many different versions of this rooster stew. Instead of pineapple juice, maize *chicha* (fermented maize drink), vinegar, or bitter orange juice can be used. The stew can also include vegetables like potatoes, carrots, and plantains, and additional meats like ham and *longaniza* or *chorizo* sausages. Sometimes carbonated drinks like Coca Cola are used for added sweetness.

Common side dishes are plantain, yuca, cheese, *crema*, and salads, and many meals include eggs and zucchini prepared in different ways. Pickled vegetables (*curtidos*) like onions, cucumbers, cabbage, beets, and tomatoes are always at the table to season all dishes to taste. Soups are common in the Salvadoran American table, including bean soups and soups that combine meats and vegetables. Rice dishes like fried rice and soupy rice are frequently served. Vegetables like *chayotes*, string beans, and *pacaya* (tender palm tree blossoms) are stuffed with cheese, dipped in egg batter, and fried. Many dishes are based on flowers like *loroco* and *izote*. *Loroco* is used in *pupusas* and *izote* is cooked with eggs, onion, and tomatoes and considered a delicacy. Leaves from a leguminous plant called *chipilín* are used as an herb or by the handful in soups and tamales. *Chipilín*, spinach, and radish leaves are mixed with eggs, tomatoes, onion, and maybe some meat to make *tortas* (fritters) that can be served in a tomato sauce with chickpeas and potatoes. A special condiment called *alguashte* is made of ground pumpkin seeds and it is sprinkled on fruits and vegetables or used as the main seasoning when cooking iguana.

Aside from *pupusas*, other tortilla-based dishes prepared by Salvadoran Americans are enchiladas and *chilaquilas*. Salvadoran enchiladas are made by frying flat maize tortillas and topping them with well-seasoned chopped meat with sauce and a topping of grated cheese, hard-boiled egg slices, and parsley. Salvadoran *chilaquilas* are made with thick tortillas that are folded or split

Eating a Salvadoran meal, New York. Courtesy of Douglas Gómez.

open and stuffed with grated cheese, tomato, and onion or with seasoned ground meat. The filled tortillas are dipped in an egg batter, fried, and dressed with onion, tomato, and vinegar. Meals can be accompanied with *atole* or *horchata*. A favorite Salvadoran dessert, called quesadillas, is a cake made with rice flour, cheese, *crema*, eggs, and sugar. Another popular dessert that is also served as an appetizer is empanadas, which are made with fried ripe plantains stuffed with sweet cream.

SOUTH AMERICANS IN THE UNITED STATES

South American cuisines can be divided into two major groups: northern South America (Bolivia, Colombia, Ecuador, Perú, and Venezuela) and southern South America, also known as the Southern Cone (Argentina, Brazil, Chile, Paraguay, and Uruguay). Northern food is characterized by Andean indigenous culinary cultures in which potatoes are as important as maize and in which spicy dishes are the norm. Southern food is distinguished by its reliance on beef, by the use of yuca as a main staple in the case of Paraguay and Brazil, and by the thorough incorporation of European foods like wine, Italian pastas, and German pastries. Inside this general pattern the cuisine of each country has its own character.

Argentinean Americans

Aside from toast with butter or jam and some ham and cheese, Argentinean Americans like for breakfast a variety of sweet pastries called *facturas* that they buy from specialized *panaderías* (bakeries). The most common ones are *medialunas* that are similar to croissants and can be made with lard or butter, and fruit tarts called *pasta frola*. Breakfast drinks can be coffee or *mate* infusion, while wine is often served with lunch or dinner.

Argentinean meals are based on meat, particularly beef. Aside from *asados* (roasted beef) and *parrillas* (grilled meats like beef ribs, steaks, organ meats, *chorizo*, and other sausages), beef is consumed in meat and vegetable stews like *carbonada criolla* and *locro* (made with hominy, beans, beef, and vegetables), in fillings for empanadas, breaded and fried in *milanesas*, and in *matambre* (literally "hunger killer"), which is flank steak rolled around a filling of vegetables and eggs. *Asados* and other dishes are accompanied by sauces like *salsa criolla* and *chimichurri*. *Salsa criolla* is made with finely chopped onion, tomatoes, red and green bell peppers, and garlic mixed with olive oil and vinegar. *Chimichurri* is a parsley sauce made with finely chopped parsley, onions, garlic, black pepper, oregano, oil, and vinegar.

Fresh, dried, and stuffed pastas and other Italian dishes like pizzas, *ñoquis* (gnocchi), and polenta are the other mainstay of the Argentine diet. Many

Facturas served at the end of an Argentine meal. Courtesy of
Natalia Policano.

of these dishes have been argentinized as is the case with pizzas. Compared
with Italian and Italian American pizzas, the basic Argentine pizza has a
thicker crust, very little tomato sauce, and lots of mozzarella cheese. One
of the most popular Argentine pizza varieties is *pizza canchera*, a cheeseless
pizza topped with well-seasoned tomato sauce. This pizza used to be sold
around stadiums in Argentina. Other Argentine favorites are grilled pizza,
stuffed pizza, and *fugaza de jamón y queso* (ham and cheese focaccia). *Fainá* is
a thin flatbread made with chickpea flour with or without cheese on top. It
is traditionally eaten with pizza, layering one slice of *fainá* on top of a slice
of pizza.

Argentines eat cookies, cakes, and pastries as snacks and as dessert, many
of them filled with dulce de leche (caramelized milk). A favorite sweet is *alfajores*, shortbread cookie sandwiches filled with dulce de leche, fruit jams, or
chocolate and covered with chocolate, white chocolate, or meringue.

Bolivian Americans

Breakfast can be coffee or tea, *marraqueta* bread with butter, jam, or cheese,
and eggs. For breakfast Bolivian Americans also enjoy *empanadas salteñas*,
turnovers stuffed with meat or chicken that are also popular as snacks and
appetizers. Potatoes are the most important element in traditional Bolivian
meals. Many dishes get a distinctive flavor from the use of an Andean hot
ají (chile) called *locoto* or *rocoto* that is available fresh, frozen, brined, and
powdered. *Locotos* are stuffed, baked, mixed into scrambled eggs, and they are

also the base of *llajua*, the table condiment that is a part of all meals. *Llajua* is made with ground *locotos*, tomatoes, and onions, and it is flavored with the Bolivian herbs *quilquiña* and *wacataya*, although in the United States they are often substituted with mint, basil, coriander, and other more easily available herbs.

Soups are a part of all meals either as a first course or as a main dish. One of the most popular soups is *sopa de maní*, made with ground peanuts and diced vegetables like potatoes and turnips. There are many varieties of *chupes* (stewlike soups), among them *chupe de pescado* (fish stew), *chupe de papalisa* (stewed *papalisa* tuber), and *chupe chuquisaqueño* that contains fresh maize, potatoes, rice, and squash. Main dishes include *picante de pollo* (chicken in a spicy sauce) and *picante mixto* (tongue, chicken, and chopped meat in a spicy sauce). These *picantes* are usually served with a side dish of *chuño phuti* made with traditionally freeze-dried potatoes cooked with onion, tomato, and scrambled eggs. Other Bolivian main dishes are *ají de lengua* (spicy tongue), *silpancho*, and *majao*. *Silpancho* is a composed dish in which a thin breaded steak is served on a bed of rice and fried potatoes, topped with a fried egg and garnished with a salad of chopped *locoto*, tomato, and onion. *Majao* is *charque* (dry meat) that has been boiled, shredded, and fried, before being mixed with cooked rice and a little broth. It is served with a fried egg on top and with fried yuca and plantains on the side. *Humintas* (fresh maize and cheese tamales also known as *humitas*) and *cuñapes* (yuca starch and cheese breads) can also be a part of a Bolivian American meal.

Brazilian Americans

Brazilian American breakfasts can include coffee, bread, pastries, ham, cheese, fresh fruits, and fruit juices. A breakfast specialty is *cuscuz nordestino*, a steamed pudding flavored with coconut milk and made with either precooked flaked cornmeal or with grated sun-dried yuca paste. Another kind of Brazilian couscous prepared for everyday meals or for parties, called *cuscuz paulista*, is a molded dish of flaked cornmeal and an assortment of stewed meats and vegetables. Brazilian meals are based on rice, beans, yuca, maize, meat, and seafood and they combine indigenous, African, and Portuguese culinary traditions, among others.

Rice is simply cooked with garlic and onions or combined with a main ingredient like shrimp, pork, dry beef, hearts of palm, sorrel leaves, or coconut milk. Common ways of preparing beans are stewed, mashed, and thickened with toasted yuca flour or flaked cornmeal, as a main ingredient in soups, and in the Bahian black-eyed pea fritters called *acarajé*. These fritters have ritual importance in the Candomblé religion but they are also a street food of widespread appeal in Bahia. They are served with a sauce made with dried and powdered shrimp heads and shells, *dendê* oil (palm oil), and hot chiles. Sometimes the fritters are split and filled with salad and with the condiments *vatapá* and *caruru*. *Vatapá* is made with ground dry shrimp, onion, garlic, roasted peanuts or cashews, bread, coconut milk, and *dendê* oil, and it can have the consistency of a sauce or of a paste. *Caruru* is a thick stew of okra, dried shrimp, ground nuts, and *dendê* oil. The dish that is considered most representative of Brazilian cuisine is a black bean stew that contains a wide variety of meats called *feijoada completa*. A traditional *feijoada completa* as made in Rio contains black beans, dried beef, salted fatback, pig tails, pig ears, pig trotters, bacon, beef tongue, pork loin, pork ribs, and sausages. It is a weekend dish meant to be shared and enjoyed leisurely. Most people vary their *feijoadas* by changing the kind of beans and the selection of meats and by adding vegetables.

Beef, grilled meats, and empanadas are as appealing to Brazilians as to Argentineans and Uruguayans. Yuca appears frequently on the Brazilian table whether fried or pureed, or as a main component of soups, breads, and croquettes. Yuca flour is fried in *dendê* oil to make a fluffy condiment called *farofa* that is sprinkled on other foods. Soups and stews are important components of a meal. There are soups, creamed vegetable soups, the popular chicken soup known as *canja*, and seafood stews called *moqueca*. Meals are rounded up with salads and cooked vegetables. Dessert can be fresh fruit or specialties like *arroz com origone* (rice with dried peaches), yuca and coconut milk pudding, and Brazil nut, coconut, or orange cakes.

Moqueca de Peixe (Brazilian Fish Stew)

2 pounds firm fish fillets
  such as cod, haddock, or
  monkfish
1 TBSP lime juice
2 TBSP peanut oil
2 TBSP *dendê* oil (palm oil)
1 juicy tomato, chopped
1 small onion, chopped

1 green bell pepper, chopped
1 red bell pepper, chopped
1/2 cup coconut milk
1/2 tsp salt
1/4 tsp pepper
4 TBSP coriander leaves,
  roughly chopped

Wash and dry the fish fillets. Sprinkle the lemon juice on the fish and set aside for 30 minutes. In a large skillet heat the oils on medium heat. Sauté the tomato, onions, and peppers for 10–15 minutes or until very soft. Add the coconut milk and simmer for 5 minutes. Add salt, pepper, fish fillets, and coriander. Cover and cook until the fish is cooked through. Serve with rice.

Chilean Americans

For breakfast Chilean Americans have tea or coffee with bread topped with jelly or *manjar* (caramelized milk). Egg dishes and cold cereals are also frequent breakfast foods. Between 4:00 P.M. and 7:00 P.M. there is a snack time called *once* in which people relax and enjoy tea or coffee and bread with jam, pâté, ham, cheese, or avocado. This meal could also include sweets like cakes, ice cream, and cookies in which case it is called *once completas*. Sometimes *once* becomes so substantial that it replaces supper and it is then known as *once-comida*. Chileans enjoy many kinds of snacks, among which the most important are empanadas (turnovers) and sandwiches. Empanadas can be baked or fried and favorite fillings are cheese, seafood, and *pino* (meat and onion). Chileans have established sandwich combinations that have their own distinctive names like *ave palta* (chicken and avocado), *ave pimienta* (chicken and red pepper), and *ave mayo* (chicken and mayonnaise). Other combinations are *Barros Luco* (steak and cheese), *chacarero* (steak, green beans, and tomatoes), and *churrasco* (marinated steak sandwiches that can include tomato slices or mashed avocado). Hot dogs are also popular and they are called *especial* when served with tomatoes and *completo* when served with all the usual trimmings.

Common starters in Chilean meals include tuna-stuffed tomatoes, *palta reina* (avocado stuffed with cubed chicken, tuna, or ham and topped with mayonnaise), and *salpicón*, a salad of cooked chicken, meat, or seafood with vegetables like potatoes, carrots, maize, and green beans. The basic Chilean salad, *ensalada chilena*, is made with sliced onions and sliced tomatoes dressed with oil, vinegar, cilantro, and salt. Other salad varieties are rice salads, bean and lentil salads, and cooked vegetable salads.

Bean and corn soups appear frequently at the traditional Chilean table. *Pancutras*, rich beef broth with fresh pasta strips, is another popular soup. The most famous Chilean soup, immortalized by the poet Pablo Neruda, is *caldillo de congrio*, a fish chowder made with conger eel. Main dishes can be grilled meats and fish, *ceviches*, and mixed seafood dishes like *mariscal* (a platter of clams, mussels, oysters, scallops, and shrimp served with a green sauce made with parsley, cilantro, and scallions) and *curanto en olla* (clambake cooked in a pot). Thin beefsteaks or pork chops *a lo pobre* ("poor man's style") are served with fried eggs, sautéed onions, and French fries. Other traditional main dishes are the spicy and aromatic seafood gratin called *chupe de jaiva*, and Chile's beloved dish, *pastel de choclo*. This dish is a pot pie that has a savory filling of chicken, beef, hard-boiled eggs, raisins, and olives, and it is topped with fresh maize pureed with butter, milk, eggs, and sugar. Chilean meals are usually complemented by table sauces like *pebre chileno*, which combines a homemade or store-bought hot red chile sauce with chopped cilantro, garlic, and onions. There is also *salsa verde* made with onions, parsley, cilantro, oil, and vinegar, and its hot version called *pebre verde*, which includes a powdered spice mixture called *merquén* that contains oregano, coriander, and smoked *ají cacho* chile. Another popular table condiment is *chancho en piedra*, a salsa that gets its name from the *piedra* or lava stone mortar and pestle in which it is made. The salsa is made by crushing garlic and chiles with salt and mixing in chopped onions, tomatoes, cilantro, oil, and vinegar. Wine is often served with Chilean meals.

For dessert Chileans like to have fresh or dried fruits and German-style tarts and cakes. One of the most popular traditional desserts is *mote con huesillos*, composed of cooked wheat berries served in a glass with dried peaches that have been poached in a syrup flavored with cinnamon, cloves, and orange zest. Another favorite is *chilenitos*, a sandwich of pastry cookies filled with *manjar* (caramelized milk) and covered with meringue.

Colombian Americans

A Colombian American breakfast can be freshly made or store-bought *arepas* with some butter or cheese, and *chorizo* sausage or eggs. Another breakfast possibility is *calentado*, which usually consists of rice and beans with some meat. *Calentado* literally means "heated," as it is usually put together with reheated leftovers. *Pandebono* and other yuca starch and cheese breads are popular Colombian breakfast treats. The most popular *arepa* for breakfast is the cheese *arepa* that has cheese mixed into the dough. Colombians from the Caribbean region have a specialty called *arepa con huevo*, which is a cooked *arepa* that is split open, stuffed with a raw egg, and fried again. A traditional breakfast from the Andes is *changua*, a milk soup with poached eggs that is seasoned with scallions and coriander leaves.

Bandeja paisa is a peasant food platter that many Colombians consider represents their cuisine. It consists of white rice, stewed red beans, *carne en polvo* (beef that has been boiled and pounded to a powder), *chicharrón*, *chorizo*, fried ripe plantain, fried egg, *arepa*, avocado, and an onion and tomato sauce called *hogao*. Stews like *ajiaco* and *sancocho* are also considered representatives of Colombian food and there are many variations of both. *Ajiaco* as made by people from Bogotá is a chicken, potato, and maize soup flavored with scallions, garlic, cilantro, and the Colombian herb called *guascas*. The soup traditionally contains two different kinds of potato, including *papa criolla*, which is indigenous to Colombia. The chicken and potatoes are cooked together until the chicken is tender and the potatoes are dissolved. Fresh maize on the cob is added to the chicken and potato broth, and the chicken is removed to be served separately in pieces or shredded. Popular *sancocho* combinations are fish with yuca, maize, and green plantains; oxtails with pumpkin, yuca,

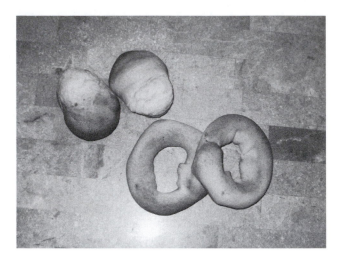

Colombian *pandebono* and *pan de queso*. Photo by Zilkia Janer.

maize, and green plantains; and chicken with onions and green plantains. The chicken *sancocho* from the city of Cartagena contains many more ingredients like beef and pork ribs, ripe and green plantains, potatoes, yuca, *ñame*, maize, cabbage, turnips, celeriac, and *auyama* squash.

Fish and seafood are enjoyed in cocktails and in coconut milk sauces. Main dishes are always served with side dishes like *chicharrón*, sliced avocado, fried or stewed yuca, and fried ripe or green plantains. Popular desserts are early figs stuffed with *arequipe* (milk caramel), *postre de natas* (milk skin sweet), and *enyucado* (coconut, cheese, and yuca cake).

Ecuadorian Americans

Among Ecuadorian Americans it is common to start the day with cereal, pancakes, waffles, or French toast, but many also enjoy savory traditional dishes for breakfast, like *ceviche* served with popcorn, *chifles* (green plantain chips), toasted maize, *ají* (hot sauce), and bread. The basic diet is composed of potatoes, rice, and meat. Lunch or dinner starts with a soup that could be a *chupe de pescado* (fish soup) or *chupe de camarones* (shrimp soup), or soups with dumplings made of cornmeal or of mashed green plantains. The thick meat and vegetable stew *sancocho* is also popular among Ecuadorians, including a fish version. *Locro*, another type of soup popular among all Andean peoples, is different from the hominy soups that have the same name in the Southern Cone. Andean *locros* are potato-based, cream-style soups that can include cheese and meat.

A favorite Ecuadorian main dish is *cazuela de verde,* a fish or shrimp pie made with a green plantain dough. Other popular dishes are *seco de chivo* (braised goat) and *seco de pollo* (braised chicken). For these dishes the goat or chicken is slowly cooked in a sauce made with onion, garlic, tomatoes, and peppers. The seasonings vary but they might include cumin, cloves, *panela* (unrefined sugar), and the cooking liquid can include beer or *chicha* (fermented drink).

Ecuadorians make different varieties of *ceviche,* including sea bass, shrimp, conch, *bacalao* (salted codfish), and chicken *ceviches.* They serve *ceviches* with plenty of its marinade, which includes tomatoes, onions, and lime, orange, or bitter orange juice. Potatoes are an important part of all meals, whether as a side dish or as the principal ingredient in main dishes. Cheese and potato patties called *llapingachos* are a favorite dish. Rice is cooked with chicken, shrimp, conch, mussels, or *chorizo* sausage, and it is also fried Chinese-style, in which case they call it *chaulafan.* Maize also has an important role in Ecuadorian meals in the form of tamales, *humitas* (fresh maize tamales), *tostado* (toasted dry maize kernels), and *mote* (hominy). *Mote* opens up like a cloud when cooked and it is served as a side dish or combined with other ingredients in stews.

Paraguayan Americans

A traditional Paraguayan breakfast consists of *mate* or *tereré* (cold infused *mate* with mint or lemongrass and sometimes with citrus juice) and *chipá* bread made with yuca starch, cheese, and egg. *Chipá* is the daily bread of Paraguayans and there are many kinds, including *chipa so'ó* made with maize flour and stuffed with meat, and *chipa guazú* made with fresh corn, cheese, and eggs.

The general diet of Paraguayans has much in common with the Argentine and Uruguayan. Grilled meats, empanadas, *milanesas* (breaded steaks), and all kinds of beef dishes are the norm. The most distinctive Paraguayan dishes come from the cuisine of the Guaraní-speaking indigenous peoples. Guaraní cuisine features yuca prominently since that was their staple before European colonization. Many of the dishes made with maize or wheat in the rest of Latin America are made with yuca in Paraguay, including tortillas and breads, fritters, *ñoquis* (gnocchi), empanadas, and sweets like *buñuelos* (yuca and cheese fritters in syrup) and *alfajores* (yuca pastries with dulce de leche filling and covered with sugar syrup). Yuca is also mixed with beef to make croquettes called *payagua mascada.* Maize is widely used in the form of hominy for stews, *mazamorra* (maize mush), and in *bori-bori* (corn flour and cheese dumplings in chicken soup). *Mbaipy-so'ó* is a dish of maize polenta with mixed-in stewed beef. Beef is paired with yuca, rice, noodles, or hominy to make a variety of stews. Two traditional dishes are *so'o yosopy* and *sopa paraguaya. So'o yosopy* is a soup made with ground beef that has been pureed in a mortar and pestle or food processor. It is served with rice or noodles mixed in or on the side. *Sopa paraguaya*, in spite of its name, is not a soup but a bread made with fresh maize and cheese.

Peruvian Americans

Peruvian breakfast can be as simple as bread and eggs or as elaborate as pork tamales with *chicharrón* and fried *camote* (Latin American sweet potato). Peruvian eating habits have been shaped by the country's incredible climatic diversity and by the ethnic diversity brought about Perú's role as the center of the Inca empire and of a Spanish colonial viceroyalty, and as the destination of immigrants from Europe, China, and Japan. Andean maize and potato dishes and *Criollo* dishes like tripe stew and *sancochos* have as much importance in Peruvian cuisine as Italian spaghetti and fettuccini, Chinese fried rice and stir-fried noodles, and Japanese sashimi and tempura.

Peruvian and Peruvian American meals are usually structured around a first and second course that might also include side dishes. Salads, *tamales*, stuffed vegetables like avocado, tomato, and *rocoto* peppers, and *ceviches* can be served as starters. Peruvian *ceviches* are made with all kinds of fish and seafood, including shrimp, conch, clams, octopus, crab, and calamari, and also with meats like chicken and duck. A simple *ceviche* is made with a single main ingredient marinated in lemon juice with hot peppers and garlic and it is served without the marinade with sides like glazed sweet potatoes, *maíz cancha* (large kernel corn), lettuce, sliced egg, and onions. Other types of ceviche are *ceviche mixto*, which combines fish with other seafood, *ceviche caliente* made with cooked chicken or shrimp, and *ceviche tiradito*, in which the fish is cut into flat slices as in sashimi instead of cubed. Another frequent starter is a potato casserole called *causa*, in which savory fillings made with tuna, shrimp, avocado, or chicken are layered between flat patties made with mashed potatoes seasoned with lemon juice, *ají amarillo* (hot yellow chiles), salt, and pepper.

Soups, stews, and chowders are an important part of Peruvian meals. Two of the most representative Peruvian soups are *chupe de camarones* (shrimp chowder made with rice, potatoes, fresh maize, cottage cheese, milk, and beaten eggs) and *parihuela* (mixed seafood soup). Second courses can be rice cooked with different kinds of meat or seafood, or refried with beans in *tacu tacu*. Meats or vegetables like maize or potatoes in spicy sauces are known as *picantes*, as in *picante de camarones* (spicy shrimp). Other main dishes are *carapulca* (freeze-dried potato casserole), *anticuchos* (marinated beef heart, fish, chicken, or beef brochettes), and *pescado a lo macho* (fish covered with shellfish in a spicy sauce). A popular dish that showcases the blending of

Andean and Chinese culinary cultures is *lomo saltado*, which is a stir-fry of beef, French fried potatoes, onion, and tomato.

Dessert can be rice pudding or a purple maize pudding known as *mazamorra morada* that contains prunes and dried peaches and is flavored with cinnamon and cloves. Another Peruvian favorite is a sweet composed of caramelized milk topped with meringue called *suspiro limeño*.

Causa Rellena de Pollo (Peruvian Potato Torte with Chicken Filling)

For the potato dough:

1 1/2 pound Yukon Gold potatoes	1 TBSP lime juice
1 TBSP *ají amarillo* paste (yellow chile paste available in jars)	2 TBSP olive oil
	1 tsp salt
	1/8 tsp black pepper

For the filling:

2 cups chicken breast, cooked and shredded	1/4 tsp black pepper
1 small onion, minced	1 avocado, thinly sliced
1/2 cup mayonnaise	Roasted red bell pepper strips and hard-boiled egg slices, to garnish
1/4 tsp salt	

Clean well the potatoes and boil them whole and unpeeled in salted water until tender. Drain and peel the potatoes when cold enough to handle. Mash the potatoes with the chile paste, lime juice, olive oil, salt, and pepper. In a separate bowl mix the shredded chicken with the onion, mayonnaise, salt, and pepper. In an oiled pie plate or baking dish, spread one-third of the potato mixture. Cover this layer with avocado slices and spread a second potato layer on top. Spread the chicken filling over the second potato layer and cover with the remaining potato mixture. Cover and refrigerate for at least 2 hours or until ready to serve. Garnish with roasted red pepper strips and hard-boiled egg slices.

Uruguayan Americans

For Uruguayan Americans breakfast is a light meal of bread with jam or butter, and coffee or *mate* infusion. A complete dinner includes bread, soup, salad, meat, cheese, wine, and fruit. Other drinks that might be served with dinner are *clericó* (white wine sangría) and *medio y medio* (a combination of a sparkling wine and white wine). Uruguayans share with Argentineans the preference for grilled beef and sausages, empanadas, pastas, and pizza.

Snack and lunch can consist of fast foods like *chivito* and *húngaras*. *Chivitos* are steak sandwiches that also include ham, Canadian bacon, pancetta, mozzarella cheese, olives, mayonnaise, *chimichurri* sauce, lettuce, tomato, and sliced hard-boiled eggs. These can be served as a sandwich or *al plato* (served on a plate without the bread and with fried potatoes). *Húngaras* are spicy sausages usually served in a hot dog bun but that are also prepared in a layered casserole with cheesy mashed potatoes. A traditional snack enjoyed with *mate* on rainy days is a fried flat bread called *torta frita*. Favorite dinner dishes are a beef tripe and chickpea or bean stew called *buseca*, and a grilled stuffed meat dish known as *pamplona*. The meat used in *pamplona* is usually chicken but pork or beef are also used. The fillings also vary but usually include ham, bacon, mozzarella cheese, red bell peppers, and hard-boiled eggs. The meat is pounded until very thin and it can be marinated in red wine, garlic, oregano, and paprika. The stuffed roll is traditionally wrapped in caul fat and grilled, but it can also be wrapped in aluminum foil and baked. Uruguayans also enjoy a variety of double-crusted savory pies like *torta pascualina* stuffed with spinach and eggs, and *torta de fiambres* stuffed with deli-thin slices of ham and mozzarella and eggs.

Among the many kinds of cakes and pastries enjoyed for dessert, *chajá* stands out for its singularity. *Chajá* is a torte made with layers of cake, meringue, Chantilly cream, dulce de leche, and peaches in syrup. The cake and meringue layers can be either in one piece or broken into pieces. The torte is finished with a layer of meringue and it is served chilled.

Venezuelan Americans

A traditional breakfast features *arepas* (maize griddle cakes) that have been cooked until crisp on both sides. Venezuelans split open their *arepas*, spread some butter inside, and stuff them with one or more ingredients like shredded meat or chicken, beans, cheese, avocado, and ripe plantains. Another common breakfast dish is scrambled eggs with onion and tomato, called *huevos pericos*. *Hallaquitas*, little plain tamales made with cornmeal and lard, are also eaten for breakfast or as a side dish. A breakfast dish common among Venezuelans from the Andes is *pisca andina*, a potato, milk, and cheese soup flavored with cilantro that is sometimes served with a poached egg on top.

The basic lunch or dinner is based on rice, beans, maize, and meat. *Pabellón criollo*, the traditional Venezuelan meal platter, consists of white rice, stewed black beans, shredded beef, and fried ripe plantains. Maize is eaten in *arepas*, *hallaquitas*, empanadas (turnovers), and *cachapas* (sweet fresh maize tamales). Rice is cooked in many different meat and vegetable combinations, and beans can be stewed, creamed, and baked. A preferred way of preparing meat is in *parrilla* (grilled). Venezuelans are also particularly fond of pasta dishes and prepare them frequently. Meals are accompanied by condiments called *ajiceros* and *mojos*. *Ajicero criollo* is made with hot chiles, oil, vinegar, pineapple or sugarcane juice, onions, cucumbers, green papaya, and carrots that are allowed to sit in a jar to merge the flavors. Another type of *ajicero*, called *ajicero de leche*, is made with hot chiles that are cooked with oregano, garlic, green onions, and red bell peppers, and mixed in a jar with boiled milk and cilantro. *Mojos* are table sauces like *mojo de leche* (milk *mojo*), made by boiling chopped onions, tomatoes, and herbs in a little milk and stirring in a few eggs until the sauce thickens. Another table sauce that is always served with grilled meats is *guasacaca*, which consists of finely chopped or liquefied avocados with garlic, onion, red bell peppers, cilantro, parsley, vinegar, oil, and salt.

Tequeños are one of the most beloved appetizers. To make these fritters, long pieces of cheese are wrapped in a thin dough made with flour, eggs, and butter. Boiled meals that combine meat and vegetables in a well-seasoned broth are served as a starter or as a main dish and they come in different combinations. The favorite one among Venezuelans from Caracas is *hervido de gallina*, made with chicken, yuca, fresh maize, *ñame* (yam), *auyama* squash, *ocuma* (taro root), and carrots. Another Caracan favorite is *asado negro*, a beef eye of round or bottom round roast that is marinated in a garlicky *adobo*. The roast is cooked in a *caldero* or Dutch oven in caramelized sugar until it gets a dark color and then it is simmered in a little water with onions and to-matoes until tender. A dish characteristic of Venezuelans from the Caribbean coast is the okra, chicken, and cabbage stew called *calalú matutero*. Venezu-elans enjoy an incredible variety of desserts, including banana bread pudding, banana cake, guava cake, and the coconut milk–soaked sponge cake called *bien me sabe* (literally "it tastes good to me").

5

Eating Out

With emigration from Latin America to the United States, many street foods and eating establishments have been transplanted to the United States, although with some changes. In Latin America, aside from restaurants that serve international and national menus, many foods are sold on public plazas, at the beach, and in food markets. There are also shops that specialize in one kind of food like pastries, bread, ceviches, *sancochos* (thick meat and vegetable stews), or *pupusas* (Salvadoran stuffed tortillas). In the United States the specialized food shops tend to broaden their offerings to include other foods that their diverse clients might want. Mexican bakeries, for example, might carry Central American breads and pastries. There are also hybrids like the *bodega/taquerías* in New York City that combine the *bodega* corner store concept with a taco shop. Many of the *bodegas* in New York that used to be managed by Cubans and Puerto Ricans are now owned by Dominican Americans and Mexican Americans, as the last two groups have grown and the first two have become more dispersed. The mixing of nationalities and concepts is an expression of how food businesses adapt as different kinds of Latin American immigrants are incorporated into the palimpsest of Latino culture.

Other changes have to do with shifts in the space and time in which specific foods are available. Because not all Latino nationalities have populations that are large and concentrated enough to sustain their own street food vendors, many foods that are considered as street or fast foods in Latin America are either not found in the United States or found in a different setting. This is the case with Puerto Rican fritters like *bacalaítos* and *alcapurrias*, which are treats that are usually sold at the beach on the island but that in New York

Versailles Restaurant, Little Havana, Miami.
Courtesy of Luis Duno Gottberg.

appear as appetizers or snacks in lunch counters and restaurants. In cases like these, the food is still available but the social context is different. The foods lose their association with spur-of-the-moment outdoors eating and become one more food to eat in the more constrained space of a restaurant. A similar change in time, space, and meaning has happened with the elaborate dishes that are usually reserved for special holidays in Latin America. Whole roasted pork, complex *moles* (meat, poultry, or fish in sauces made with ground nuts, chiles, and spices), rich desserts and other dishes that used to be prepared only for Christmas, Lent, and family celebrations have become available all year-round. The dishes become disconnected from the calendar of celebrations and lose some of their festive appeal.

Food plays an important role in the construction of identity, and as a new identity is being forged, a new food culture is also created. Latin American food cultures have changed in the process of becoming Latino, but the creation of a Latino food culture does not imply a rupture with the Latin American ones. The constant flow of people between the United States and Latin America has allowed Latino and Latin American food cultures to remain connected and impact each other as both keep changing. Interestingly, many Latin Americans are surprised to see that many foods and eating habits that they consider close to extinction in their countries survive among Latinos. With the rapid urbanization of Latin America, many traditional ways of cooking and eating are being abandoned, while in the United States, because of nostalgia and the political need to assert Latino identities, there seems to be more of a stake in conserving them.

The Latino eating out experience revolves around markets, bakeries, and different kinds of restaurants, street foods, and fast foods. In each case it can be seen that there is a tendency to cross boundaries of nationality and of concept. This boundary crossing is indeed the trademark of Latino identity and culture.

MARKETS

Traditional markets in Latin America are large spaces where vendors of all kinds of merchandise come together. Going to the market is a social occasion in which the family spends the day getting groceries, household supplies, or clothes, and eating at one of the many food stands. In the United States, Latino food businesses and businesses that cater to Latinos have tried to reproduce the experience of shopping at the market. For Latinos, shopping for groceries is one more kind of food-related sociability.

In New York, in the neighborhood known as *El Barrio* or Spanish Harlem, the open air market known as *La Marqueta* transported Puerto Rican and other Latino customers back home for a few hours with its well-stocked stalls full of fresh fruits, vegetables, grains, and meat cuts that were not generally available. These days only a small section of *La Marqueta* is open and it is no longer the main place where Latinos buy their groceries. This is in part due to the fact that many Latino ingredients like yuca, plantains, avocados, mangoes, and cilantro have become mainstream enough to be found anywhere. It is also due to the proliferation of many smaller independent Latino entrepreneurs that adapt to the changing Latino community more efficiently. *Bodegas*, the corner stores that together with *La Marqueta* used to be the only place to get hard-to-find Latino ingredients, have also lost that role. In fact, *bodegas* in *El Barrio* carry mostly the cheapest processed foods and malt liquor characteristic of any economically depressed neighborhood in the United States. The Moore Street Market in Brooklyn, nicknamed *la marketa de Williamsburg,* is more alive but its 16 independent vendors have been threatened with eviction to make space for an affordable housing building. People come to this *marketa* to shop for fresh fruits and vegetables from Puerto Rico, the Dominican Republic, and México, and to eat at its coffee shop and restaurant. There they can also find meat, ice cream, flowers, Puerto Rican souvenirs, a beauty parlor, an old-fashioned barber shop, a Latin music store, and a *botánica* (a shop that supplies herbs and other items for the practice of the Afro-Caribbean religion called *santería*).

In Texas and California there are more successful open air markets. Historic Market Square in San Antonio is a tourist attraction but it still provides the full food shopping and eating experience found in Mexican markets. In the Grand Central Public Market, Los Angeles' oldest and largest open air market, Mexican and other Latinos can shop for bulk foods like dried maize, beans, rice, chile peppers, and spices. There they can also find fresh Latin

American breads, tortillas, seafood, and meats, including fish fresh enough for *ceviche* (citrus-marinated raw seafood pieces), homemade *chorizos* and other sausages, and hard-to-find meat cuts and specialty parts. This market also offers other important services like check cashing, telephone cards, and money transfers. The market experience is complete with food stands that offer everything from tacos and other Mexican snacks to *pupusas, ceviches,* and fresh fruit juices.

If open air markets are not as many or as successful as they used to be, the multiethnic supermarket seems to be a rising trend. Multiethnic supermarkets combine the format of large supermarkets with produce and food products from all over the world. Some of the most popular chain supermarkets that follow this trend are Trade Fair in New York, Liborio Markets in California and Nevada, and Fiesta Mart in Texas. Supermarkets like these carry all of the same products found in regular supermarkets plus foods from Latin America, the Caribbean, Asia, and Africa, according to the specific ethnic composition of their location. However, freshness is not the strongest point of some of the supermarkets of this kind, given the wide range of produce that they attempt to stock. Many fruits and vegetables remain displayed past their peak because of their slow turnover rate. Tortillas, fresh cheeses, creams, and bakery goods are usually reasonably fresh, although not compared with the same products bought in specialty shops.

The more attractive aspects of multiethnic supermarkets are one-stop shopping convenience and imported products that can stand long storage. Fruits and vegetables that do not travel well enough to be imported profitably like guavas, *guanábana* (soursop), and *mamey* (an orange-fleshed fragrant fruit) are found frozen or in syrup. The frozen section also carries fruit pulps to make *batidos* (fruit milkshakes) and frozen root vegetables that are already peeled and cut up. Other foods available in the frozen section are plantain leaves, *papa criolla* (a Colombian potato variety), *papa amarilla* (a Peruvian potato variety), and Andean *rocoto* peppers. They also stock cans with all kinds of beans, boiled hominy, and ready-made stews like *mondongo* and *pozole*. The still-strong Goya brand shares shelf space with brands imported from México and other countries. There is also a wide range of imported sodas, fruit juices, candies, cookies, and crackers. A large section is always devoted to dry beans and to flours like yuca flour, yuca starch, plantain flour, cracked wheat, cornstarch, maize, and precooked maize products for *arepas* (maize griddle cakes), tortillas, and tamales. Heat-and-eat foods, bottled condiments, salsas, *moles,* and instant mixes for drinks and desserts are also popular. Many multiethnic supermarkets also have a *taquería* (taco shop) or a hot deli with ready-to-eat meals to eat in or take out.

Many Latinos insist on buying only the freshest ingredients to cook at home so they patronize small specialized shops. They depend on neighborhood *fruterías* to buy both regular and specialty produce. Fruits sold include mangoes, different varieties of avocado, tamarind, guavas, and *tunas* (prickly pears). Among the vegetables there are poblano chiles, sweet chiles (*ajicitos*), long leaf cilantro (*culantro* or *recao*), young cactus paddles (*nopalitos*), different kinds of bananas, plantains, and root vegetables. Butcher shops (*carnicerías*) provide the wide variety of meat cuts and parts used in Latino cooking. Seafood shops (*pescaderías*) offer fish and shellfish fresh enough for *ceviche* and many also sell seafood stews and cocktails. *Viveros* (live poultry shops) are the place to find live chickens as well as older hens, guinea fowl, and other birds that are slaughtered to order.

Another way to secure Latino foods and ingredients is by Internet shopping. Special orders of fresh fruits in season, prepared tamales, and other delicacies are attainable, thanks to next-day delivery services. Some Latinos also receive food and ingredients from friends and relatives in Latin America, and most bring back suitcases full of food and ingredients when they visit Latin America.

BAKERIES

Latino bakeries, or *panaderías*, sell the breads and pastries that people are used to buying for breakfast and for dessert in Latin America, as well as some of the pastries found in other bakeries in the United States. Latinos tend to be partial to the breads and pastries from their or their family's countries of origin. One neighborhood can have many bakeries because each one is identified with a specific nationality or region. The Latinos that have the strongest presence in the bakery business are Argentineans, Brazilians, Colombians, Cubans, Dominicans, Guatemalans, Mexicans, and Salvadorans, although it is possible to find bakeries of every nationality and many Latino bakeries carry breads and pastries from more than one national origin. Most bakeries also sell a wide variety of foods and drinks for breakfast, lunch, and dinner. Bakeries are lively places with people constantly coming in and out. Customers come in the morning for breakfast breads and pastries to take home or eat in and keep coming throughout the day for quick lunches and snacks. Bakeries are open late for people who buy desserts to take home.

Argentinean American bakeries specialize in desserts filled with dulce de leche (caramelized milk) and in empanadas (small flaky turnovers) with a variety of fillings. Jelly rolls, *alfajores* (cookie sandwiches), and many *facturas* (pastries) are filled with the creamy caramelized milk that is a favorite among South Americans in the United States. *Facturas* are also filled with *membrillo* (quince) paste and with guava and cheese. Another popular item is *masitas*, small sugar cookies topped with maraschino cherries, nuts, jams, or chocolate. On the savory side, aside from empanadas, there are tortillas (Spanish omelettes), *tartas* (quiches), and tea sandwiches made with crustless white

Mexican breads. Clockwise from top left: *bolillo, concha,* and *pan de muerto* (bread of the dead). Photo by Zilkia Janer.

bread called *sandwiches de miga*. Other sandwiches usually sold in Argentinean American bakeries are *choripan* and *pebete*. *Choripan* is a grilled sandwich of *chorizo* sausage in a baguette, and *pebete* refers to a spongy oval bun with a thin crust used to make sandwiches with a filling of cheese, cured meats, and tomato. Argentinean bakeries usually carry *yerba mate* (*mate* leaves to make infusions). Many bakeries have space to sit down and eat in, although the norm is to take the food home for breakfast, tea, or supper.

Empanadas (South American Savory Flaky Turnovers)

For the dough:
1 1/2 cups wheat flour
1/2 tsp baking powder
1/2 tsp salt
6 TBSP butter or lard
1/3 cup water

1/2 tsp salt
1/2 pound beef, finely
  minced with a knife, or
  ground beef
1 tsp sweet paprika
1 tsp ground cumin

For the filling:
1 TBSP olive oil
2 medium onions, chopped
2 garlic cloves, minced
1 bay leaf

1/2 tsp dry oregano
Hot chile sauce to taste
1/2 cup warm broth or water
1/2 TBSP flour
2 hard-boiled eggs, chopped

Mix the flour, salt, and baking powder in a food processor. Add the butter or lard cut in small pieces and process until no large pieces can be seen. With the machine running, add enough of the water through the chute until the mixture begins to be gathered into a ball. Knead lightly by hand for 1 minute and refrigerate the dough wrapped in plastic wrap for 30 minutes.

Heat the oil in a skillet and sauté the onion and garlic with the bay leaf until soft. Add the beef and cook until it loses its pink color. Add salt, paprika, cumin, oregano, and hot sauce, and cook, stirring constantly for 1 minute. Add the water and let boil until some of it has been absorbed. Stir in the flour and cook for 1 minute. Remove the bay leaf and mix in the hard-boiled eggs. Taste to adjust the seasonings and refrigerate the filling for at least 30 minutes.

Divide the dough into six equal parts and shape them into balls. Roll each ball into 6 1/2 inch circles. Place 2 tablespoons of filling in one-half of each circle and fold the other half over the filling. Lightly moisten the edges with a little water and press them together to seal. Use a fork to crimp the edges and to pierce the tops. Bake in a 375° oven for 20 minutes and let rest for 5 minutes before serving.

The most popular item in Brazilian American bakeries is *pão de queijo*, cheese and yuca starch buns that have a moist and chewy interior. The bakeries also sell *pasteles* (turnovers) with chicken, shrimp, or hearts of palm fillings, and a variety of sandwiches, including pastry sandwiches filled with ham and cheese, spinach, or hearts of palm. A popular snack is *coxinhas*, or mock chicken legs. *Coxinhas* are deep-fried croquettes made with a thin potato and wheat flour dough that is filled with diced chicken and Brazilian cream cheese and shaped like a teardrop to resemble a chicken leg. Other popular snacks sold in Brazilian bakeries are of Middle Eastern origin, like *quibe* (bulgur and meat croquettes) and *esfiha* (baked turnovers filled with beef or spinach and cheese). Brazilian sweets feature coconut prominently, as well as other fruits like guava and passion fruit. One of the many coconut desserts is *quindim*, a yellow custard made with egg yolks, sugar, and ground coconut. Egg yolk desserts of Portuguese origin like *papo de anjo* are another specialty. To make this dessert, baked whipped egg yolks are shaped by hand and briefly boiled in sugar syrup that can be flavored with rum or vanilla. The egg yolks are served in the syrup either chilled or at room temperature. Another dessert commonly found in Brazilian bakeries is called *brigadeiros*, which are trufflelike balls made of condensed milk, butter, and chocolate. Most bakeries also sell fresh tropical fruit juices.

Colombian bakeries in the United States are known for yuca starch and cheese breads called *pandebonos*, which can be shaped like rolls or rings.

A similar cheese and yuca dough that is shaped like a ball and deep fried is called *buñuelo*. Other Colombian bakery favorites are *arepas* (griddle maize cakes), *chorizo* and other sausages, fried ripe plantain slices with white cheese, and empanadas (turnovers). Many of the sweets are filled with *arequipe* (caramelized milk), guava paste, or both. Early figs stuffed with caramelized milk (*brevas con arequipe*) are one of the favorite sweets. Other favorites are *pastel gloria* (puff pastry filled with guava paste) and *torta negra* (a fruit and nut cake covered with royal icing that is sought after for Christmas). Flan, bread pudding, and sugar cookies are also favorites. One of the most popular Colombian desserts sold in bakeries and even in their own specialized shops is the icy fruit treats called *cholados*. To make cholados a glass is filled with shaved ice, fruit syrup, and cut-up pieces of fresh fruits like mango, pineapple, melon, banana, and apple. The glass is finally topped with condensed milk and sometimes also with coconut flakes or ice cream. A similar preparation is a drink called *salpicón de frutas*, which is a combination of fresh fruits and cola champagne soda topped with condensed milk. Another Colombian drink available at some bakeries is *champús*. This drink is made with boiled and ground dried maize mixed with unrefined cane sugar, cloves, cinnamon, finely chopped pineapple, and *lulo* fruit pulp. *Lulo*, also known as *naranjilla*, is a tart juicy fruit, which is widely consumed in the form of juice. Another Colombian drink is *masato*, a slightly fermented drink made of cooked rice or maize meal, flavored with unrefined cane sugar, cloves, cinnamon, and orange leaves.

Arepas de Queso (Colombian Cheese and Maize Griddle Cakes)

1 cup *arepa* flour (pre-cooked cornmeal)	1 1/2 cups warm water
1/2 tsp salt	1/2 cup grated mozzarella or Muenster cheese

In a large bowl mix the flour and salt. Add the water and stir to form a soft dough. Cover and let it rest for 5 minutes. Add the grated cheese and knead for 2 minutes or until smooth. Divide the dough into 4 equal pieces and shape them into balls. Flatten the balls into 1/4 inch thick disks between your hands or on the countertop using a flat plate and keeping the dough between two pieces of plastic wrap. Heat a heavy or cast iron skillet over medium heat and grease it lightly with oil or butter. Cook the *arepas* for 12 to 15 minutes, turning them a couple of times until a crust forms on both sides. Serve hot.

Pandebono (Colombian Yuca and Cheese Bread Rolls)

1 cup grated *queso fresco*
  (white farmer's cheese)
1/4 cup yuca starch
1 TBSP precooked
  cornmeal

1 tsp sugar
1/4 tsp salt
1/2 tsp baking powder
1 egg, slightly beaten
Water as needed

In a food processor, mix the cheese, yuca starch, cornmeal, sugar, salt, and baking powder. With the machine running, add the egg and enough water for the mixture to form a soft ball. Scoop dough with a tablespoon and form into balls. Place on a lightly greased baking sheet and bake in a 425° oven for 12–15 minutes. Serve warm. Makes 8 small *pandebonos*.

Cuban American bakeries are the place to get Cuban coffee, bread, pastries, and sweets. Many of them also offer full breakfast, lunch, dinner, and catering services. Among the sweets there are popular Latino desserts like flan, *churros* (fried pastry strips), meringues, and cakes soaked in brandy-flavored syrup with custard or fruit fillings. A popular Cuban cake called *capuchino* is a cone-shaped sponge cake soaked in syrup. Flaky turnovers—called *pasteles* or *pastelitos* by Cubans, *empanaditas* or *pastelitos* by Dominicans, and *pastelillos* by Puerto Ricans—are filled with sweet fillings like guava, cream cheese, or coconut, and with savory fillings like ham or meat. Other savory specialties include *cangrejitos* (crescent-shaped pastries filled with ham or *chorizo*), ham, cheese, chicken, or codfish croquettes, *papas rellenas* (meat-stuffed potato croquettes) and Cuban tamales. The latter are made with ground fresh maize with a savory filling of diced chicken or meat mixed into the batter. Cuban American bakeries also offer a wide variety of sandwiches from the well-known *cubano* and *medianoche* sandwiches that are filled with roast pork, ham, and Swiss cheese, to more recent innovations like *papa preparada* and *croqueta preparada*. *Papa preparada* is a sandwich with a filling of flattened *papa rellena*, Swiss cheese, and lettuce, and *croqueta preparada* is filled with flattened *croquetas*, Swiss cheese, and ham. Bakeries are a gathering place for Cubans in Miami and many serve unofficially as meeting points for political activists. The famous Versailles restaurant and bakery has for decades been considered not only as the best place to find old-style Cuban food, but also as an obligatory stop for campaigning politicians and as the place where news reporters go to gauge reactions to events related to Cuba.

Dominican American bakeries sell bread and sweet and savory *pastelitos* (turnovers) as well as sandwiches, ham and cheese croissants, and desserts like flan, cheesecake, donuts, *mantecados* (crumbly butter biscuits), cupcakes, and bread pudding. However, the main attraction at these bakeries is the Dominican cakes that are an indispensable part of all family celebrations. They are buttery layer cakes with a baked-in filling. The filling can be guava, pineapple, strawberry, dulce de leche, or vanilla or chocolate custard. The cakes are decorated with colorful meringue icing to suit all occasions. Bakery windows display white heart-shaped cakes to celebrate anniversaries, book-shaped cakes to celebrate first communions, cradle-shaped cakes for baby showers, and cakes with sports and animated character themes for birthdays. The demand for these cakes is so great that many people have set up successful home businesses baking cakes by special order.

Bakeries that sell Guatemalan breads carry French bread, a wide variety of sweet breads, eggy *pan de yemas*, orange or apple *cubiletes* (muffins), and banana quick bread. *Champurrado*, a round and flat baking powder bread similar to a scone, is a treat that many Guatemalans enjoy dipping in their coffee. Another Guatemalan favorite is *marquesotes*, airy cakes made with whipped egg whites, egg yolks, butter, sugar, and very little flour and cornstarch. Guatemalan quesadilla is like a coffee cake made with wheat and rice flour, sour cream, and dry cheese. The bakeries also sell empanadas (turnovers) with fruit fillings like guava and strawberry. Some bakeries serve breakfast, lunch platters, and snacks like Guatemalan enchiladas, tostadas, tacos, and *pan con chile* (stuffed chile sandwich).

Mexican American bakeries carry French bread rolls, *bolillos* (crusty bread rolls for sandwiches), and sweet breads in many different shapes. A popular sweet bread is *concha*, which is shaped like a domed seashell and has a crunchy sugar topping. Another favorite is the crescent-shaped *cuernito* that sometimes has a fruit jam filling. Corn bread is made with fresh maize and it is usually shaped like an ear of corn. Fancier sweet breads enriched with dried fruits, nuts, and spices are made for special holidays like *pan de muerto* for the Day of the Dead, and *rosca de Reyes* for Three Kings Day. Donuts and birthday cakes are also regular items. Mexican bakeries often serve breakfast and light meals.

Salvadoran American bakeries sell *pupusas*, French bread rolls, and *torta de yema*, a briochelike loaf bread that is used to make *torrejas* (French toast). They also have coffee cakes like quesadillas made with cheese and sour cream, and *semita*, which is a flat sweet bread with guava or pineapple filling. Other Salvadoran favorites are the sponge cake called *marquesote*, a fruit- or cream-filled layered cake called *María Luisa*, and the rum and cinnamon syrup–soaked cakes known as *borrachos*. Puff pastry is presented in different shapes and fillings, like *relámpagos* that have a lightning bolt shape and a cream filling, and *herraduras* that have a horseshoe shape and a fruit filling.

Pupusas (Salvadoran Stuffed Tortillas)

1 cup instant corn *masa*
  flour (*Maseca* or *Masa*
  Harina)
1/2 cup warm water

1/2 cup *queso blanco* or
  mozzarella, grated
1/2 cup chilled refried beans
1 1/2 TBSP vegetable oil

Mix the flour and water and add more water as necessary to form a moist dough that does not crack at the edges when pressed down. Let the dough rest for 5 minutes and divide it into 4 equal parts. Shape each part into a ball and make an indentation in the middle with your thumb to form a cup. Place 2–3 teaspoons of cheese and/or beans in the cup, packing it down slightly. Close the cup by closing your hand to stretch the dough over to enclose the filling. Shape the dough again into a ball and flatten it to a thickness of 1/4 inch between two sheets of plastic wrap using a flat-bottomed plate. Alternatively, divide each ball of dough into two small balls and flatten them into thin disks with a rolling pin. Spread the filling on one disk and cover with a second disk, pressing to seal the edges. Lightly oil both sides of the *pupusas* and cook them for 5 minutes on each side on a heavy or cast iron skillet over medium heat, turning frequently. They are cooked when blistered and slightly puffed. Serve with *curtido* and any hot tomato sauce.

Curtido (Salvadoran Pickled Cabbage and Carrots)

3 cups cabbage, shredded
1/2 cup carrots, shredded
1/4 cup scallions, thinly
  sliced

1/4 cup white vinegar
1/4 cup water
1 tsp dried oregano
1/2 tsp red pepper flakes

In a large saucepan bring 2 cups of water to a boil and remove from the heat. Add the cabbage and carrots, soak for 5 minutes, and drain. Mix all the ingredients in a nonreactive bowl, cover, and refrigerate for at least 6 hours before serving.

RESTAURANTS

Many Latinos report that when eating out they prefer Chinese food, pasta, and salads, and that they never go to restaurants that serve the food from their or their family's home country. The food in such restaurants is never good enough compared to the food that they remember and that many still cook at home. These judgments can be the result of nostalgia for an idealized past, but they also reflect the reality of restaurants run more out of necessity than out of inclination, training, or talent. Still the restaurants thrive because by serving the different national Latino foods they serve many different needs. Many Latino workers that do not have the time, knowledge, or facilities to cook at home eat many of their meals in inexpensive neighborhood restaurants that serve homestyle food. Other Latinos might choose to patronize a food business because it provides the opportunity to socialize with other Latinos of the same nationality, because they are often the only place where street foods that are not normally cooked at home can be found, and because they help introduce younger generations to the foods that they might not know.

There are many different kinds of Latino restaurants. Cafeterias, *mesones*, and *fondas* sell quick meals like sandwiches and a few daily specials of homestyle food. Juice bars (*juguerías*) sell refreshing fresh fruit juices and milkshakes that people enjoy any time of day. Other establishments specialize in a specific kind of prepared foods to eat on the go or to take home. Puerto Ricans patronize snack shops called *cuchifritos*. These shops sell Puerto Rican fritters like *bacalaítos* (codfish fritters), *alcapurrias* (grated green plantain fritters with a ground meat filling), *rellenos de papa* (mashed potato fritters with a ground meat filling), and *sorullitos* (cornmeal sticks). *Cuchifrito* shops often are combined with *lechoneras* that sell roasted pig with crispy skin by the pound. They also sell *chicharrón* (pork rind), *mondongo* (pork tripe stew), and other dishes made with pork innards. Other popular Latino take-out food shops are rotisserie shops, or *rotiserías* that specialize in roasted meat and chicken and dishes to accompany them. Spicy marinated Peruvian rotisserie chickens are especially popular.

Full-service restaurants, usually associated with one specific nationality, feature dishes that represent different regions of a country, including snacks and festive foods. Many restaurants combine a full menu with a specialization in the given country's iconic food. Venezuelan restaurants in this country, for example, advertise as *areperías* (*arepa* shops) that also serve full Venezuelan meals. Salvadoran restaurants in the United States often are little more than *pupuserías* (*pupusa* shops) that offer a few other dishes, and some Ecuadorian and Peruvian restaurants in this country identify themselves as *cevicherías* (*ceviche* shops), even though they often have more extensive menus.

Argentinean and Brazilian restaurants are predominantly steakhouses called *parrillas* and *churrascarias*, respectively. There is more to all of these cuisines than their iconic foods but there is not enough of a market to sustain full-menu restaurants that specialize in only one Latino nationality.

Mexican restaurants are the clearest example of how difficult it is for an immigrant cuisine to avoid being reduced to a few iconic snack foods. *Taquerías* (taco shops) originated as street fast foods in México but there is a popular misconception in the United States that Mexican cuisine is limited to their local *taquería* menu. Traditional taco shops specialize in the time-consuming meat preparations that are eaten wrapped in a tortilla. These include *carne asada* (marinated grilled beef), *carnitas* (pork meat that has been braised, shredded, and roasted or fried), *barbacoa* (slow cooked meats including head meat), and *carne al pastor* (marinated rotisserie pork), among many others. These meats can also be served in sandwiches called *tortas*. *Taquerías* in the United States are likely to also sell *burritos*, the rice, beans, and meat meals wrapped in a large wheat flour tortilla that is the trademark of U.S.-México border food. Many *taquerías* use the U-shaped hard corn taco shells that are rarely seen in México. Fortunately, there is an increasing diversity of Mexican food establishments. These include *tortillerías* (tortilla shops) that sell freshly made tortillas and *masa* (nixtamalized maize dough) to make tamales, *tamalerías* (shops that sell tamales) that increasingly include tamales from other Latin American countries, and *birrierías* that specialize in goat stew. There are also several high-end Mexican restaurants run by professional chefs that explore the richness of regional Mexican cuisines and present them in a fine dining context. As a Latino middle class becomes established, there are better conditions for more fine dining Latino restaurants. The most successful of these enterprises are pan-Latino or Nuevo Latino restaurants that are patronized by middle-class Latinos and by non-Latinos. However, such restaurants have been welcomed by Latinos more because of their refined atmosphere than because of their food. Many Latinos are disappointed with how pan-Latino restaurants reinterpret classic dishes and consider that the new versions are of inferior quality because they do not respect Latino taste preferences to cater to the wider and generally more affluent Anglo American clientele.

FOOD ON WHEELS

In Latino neighborhoods food is sold on the streets at key times and places. Food is sold from trucks that park on busy streets on weekends and on weekdays during the after-work rush hours. Pushcarts and even supermarket carts located close to mass transit stops are used to offer a quick bite to people

Taco truck, New York. Photo by Zilkia Janer.

on the go. On weekends the vendors can be seen selling snacks late into the night to people coming out of nightclubs and late work shifts. Soccer matches organized by Latino soccer leagues are another place where food vendors come to sell the foods that complete the sports event atmosphere. The soccer fields and the streets of Latino neighborhoods have acquired the role that public plazas have in Latin America: a place to unwind, meet with friends, and enjoy a snack.

The food sold in Latino neighborhoods depends on the specific ethnic composition of the neighborhood. Mexican Americans sell tacos, *champurrado* (chocolate and maize drink), *churros,* and all kinds of *antojitos* (snacks) like *tortas,* gorditas, *huaraches,* and *sopes.* Many varieties of *tamales* are sold on the street by Mexican American and Central American women that sell their own regional varieties. Empanadas are another popular street food found in many different versions. Dominican *chimichurri* trucks, not to be confused with the Argentine parsley sauce of the same name, sell seasoned hamburger patties on a roll with cabbage, tomato, and mayonnaise salad. Other Dominican American vendors sell *morir soñando* (orange juice milkshakes), *chicharrón* to be savored with a squirt of lime, the sweet bean dessert *habichuelas con dulce,* yuca dough empanadas called *cativías,* and *quipes* (bulgur and meat fritters). Vendors from Ecuador sell *ceviche* with all the fixings, and those from Colombia sell cornmeal and fresh maize *arepas.* Cuban Americans sell their own hamburger version called *frita,* which is a seasoned ground pork and beef patty in a hamburger bun with crispy thin potato sticks.

Selling banana leaf–wrapped tamales at a street fair, New York. Photo by Zilkia Janer.

Morir Soñando (Dominican Orange Juice Milkshake)

2 cups orange juice   2 cups ice cubes
1 1/2 cups evaporated milk   1/4 cup sugar if desired

Combine all the ingredients in a blender and liquefy until smooth and creamy. Serve immediately.

In all cases there is plenty of fresh fruit juices, drinks, ice creams, and *paletas* (fruit pops). Orange juice, sugarcane juice, coconut water, and fresh fruit shakes are made to order. Shaved ice cones, called *piraguas, raspados, frío fríos,* or *nieves,* are topped with fruit-flavored syrups or with caramelized milk. Roasted corn on the cob is dressed with a sprinkle of salt, chile powder, and lime juice. Fresh fruits are sold in convenient and attractive ready-to-eat arrangements. Mangoes are peeled, carved to resemble a flower, and stuck on a stick. Mango slices and other cut-up fruits in plastic bags are ready to receive salt, chile, and lime to the taste of the customer. Almost anytime, anywhere, there is Latino food on the street to satisfy all kinds of cravings.

Arepas for sale at a street fair, New York. Photo by Zilkia Janer.

FAST-FOOD CHAINS

Fast-food chains like Taco Bell, Taco Maker, and Chipotle sell Mexican food adapted to mainstream Anglo American taste, and they have never been popular among Latinos. Now fast-food chains from Latin America have started to open franchises in the United States to cater to the millions of Latinos that are not adequately served by Anglo American fast-food chains. Pollo Campero, a Guatemalan chain specializing in crispy and spicy chicken has franchises in 11 countries all over the world, including the United States where it already has 35 restaurants. Central American immigrants who were not satisfied with Kentucky Fried Chicken and used to bring back Pollo Campero chickens in their suitcases when visiting their home countries alerted the company to the possibilities of growth in the United States. Gorditas Doña Tota, a Mexican chain specializing in gorditas (fat maize tortillas stuffed with a variety of meats and stews), has opened a restaurant in Texas. Mexican taco chains like Taco Inn (which has franchises in Guatemala, Salvador, and Honduras) and El Fogoncito (with restaurants in Costa Rica, Honduras, and Nicaragua) are planning to open outlets in the United States in the near future. Even Latin American fast-food chains that do not sell Latin American food have decided to enter the Latino food market in the United States, as is the case with the Mexican chain of Japanese restaurants called Sushi Itto that has outlets in Central America and Europe and has already opened two restaurants in California. The Brazilian chain Habib's, which serves Arab foods, is also planning to establish itself in the United States. Latino food is not only a collection of foods and ingredients but also a culinary point of view from which fast foods and world cuisines are reinterpreted.

6

Special Occasions

Throughout the year there are many Latino family, religious, national, and community celebrations that break up the daily routine and bring people together. Food is an important part of all celebrations and oftentimes it defines their mood and character. Latino celebrations vary by ethnicity, social class, region, and available financial resources. Not all Latinos celebrate the same holidays, and they do not celebrate the same holidays in the same way. Latino ways of celebrating with food have also become different from Latin American ones as holidays and food are one more terrain in which Latinos negotiate their identity in the United States.

The date on which some holidays are celebrated has been shifted to better fit the work calendar in the United States. This is why carnival, which began as a party of excess right before the beginning of the abstinence period of Lent, is celebrated on Memorial Day weekend in the Mission District in San Francisco and why many other celebrations like patron saint days are observed during the weekend closest to the original date. The creation of an official Hispanic Heritage Month from September 15 to October 15 has resulted in the concentration of Latino cultural festivals organized by educators and government and nongovernment organizations during this period. Such festivals are intended to serve as educational tools for outsiders and often fail to resonate with Latino communities that prefer to celebrate their holidays according to their own calendar and logic.

There have also been changes in the meaning of some of the celebrations. Festivals that were generally reserved for religious devotees or for nationalist activists become more widely celebrated in the United States. Nonreligious Latinos join religious festivities as a way of asserting their cultural identity and as a way of meeting other Latinos. Even festivities related to specific nationalities like the Mexican Cinco de Mayo have become pan-Latino and even mainstream celebrations that attract Latinos and non-Latinos alike. Almost all celebrations, regardless of their intended main purpose, are occasions in which Latino foods are celebrated and showcased, although as events grow in popularity and become mainstream events with corporate sponsorship, mainstream foods become more present.

Latinos have in turn adopted and adapted the major holidays celebrated in the United States. Fourth of July and Thanksgiving Day are widely observed since they are official holidays that most people can take off, but Latinos have given new meanings to these celebrations. The Fourth of July is a hopeful date for all the documented and undocumented Latinos that struggle to realize their own dreams of freedom and equality in this country. Thanksgiving and Columbus Day (transformed into *Día de la Raza*) have become occasions to reflect on the continued subordination of indigenous peoples and cultures in the Americas. The foods served during these holidays reflect the negotiations and the fluidity of Latino identity. A Latino Fourth of July barbecue might include marinated roasted meats, hamburgers seasoned with *adobo*, and hot dogs dressed up with avocado, onions, cheese, or potato sticks. The Thanksgiving turkey might be flavored with a garlicky rub or spicy sauce, stuffed with plantain *mofongo*, yuca, or *congris* (red beans and rice), or altogether substituted with a roasted pork leg. The side dishes are likely to be traditional Latin American foods like *tamales*, *pasteles*, beans, and rice or tortillas.

Most Latino celebrations share a core of festive foods that is specific to each country or region, but there are also holidays that require their own distinctive foods. The celebrations and their corresponding foods can be classified into feasting, fasting, and feeding spiritual life.

FEASTING

Weekend meals are generally more elaborate and festive than regular weekday meals. Sundays are the day when many Latinos like to take the whole family out for dinner at a full-service restaurant. In the summer months in New York many Latinos enjoy going out for seafood soups. In south Texas Mexicans wait for Sundays to enjoy their *barbacoas* (pit-roasted meats, whole kid, or cow's head). Along the U.S.-México border and in towns with large Mexican populations all over the United States, neighborhood shops sell *menudo* (spicy tripe soup) on Sunday and many people look for it after Sunday mass. Organ meat dishes, which remain popular for family celebrations in border towns among working-class Mexicans, are a symbol of their cultural survival as many of their ranch-style foods have been appropriated by mainstream culture.[1] The best example of this appropriation is probably the case of fajitas that originated as the ranchers' way of flavoring and tenderizing the inexpensive and rejected diaphragm muscle of steers but that has become a best-selling item in Mexican restaurants that cater to the general public. Now that cut of meat has become too expensive for working-class Mexicans.

Latino extended families often get reunited during the weekend for a festive meal. Sharing a weekend meal is also a way of binding together extended surrogate families and communities of workers that are away from their biological families. In rural settlements where migrant farm workers spend the off-season, they get together in groups to cook and share food as a way of stretching their scarce resources and of saving their dignity in their often-degrading situation.[2] In similar situations in urban and suburban contexts, where Latino workers live in crowded homes with family and nonfamily members, Sunday get-togethers are common. They prepare and share a *sancocho* (thick meat and vegetable stew) or any meal that gives them a sense of celebration and of community.

Life cycle events are occasions that are celebrated with reunions around food. When a baby is born, it is customary for the parents to give away sweets (and cigars in the case of baby boys) to spread the news. After a baptism ceremony, the family of the baby and the godparents break bread together and offer a party in which sweets abound. Sweets made with eggs like meringues and *yemitas* (sweetened egg yolks) are preferred because eggs symbolize life and the baptized baby has just started life anew as a Christian. Birthdays are

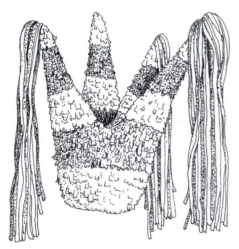

Piñata. © J. Susan Cole Stone.

celebrated with colorful cakes and with *piñatas* filled with toys, candy, and confetti. *Piñatas* are paper containers in a variety of shapes and decorated with brightly colored tissue. The *piñata* is suspended from a tree branch or from the ceiling, and blindfolded kids take turns trying to break it with a stick. A highlight of the birthday party is when the *piñata* breaks and it showers everybody with its colorful bounty.

The most significant birthday among Latinas is the 15th birthday or *quinceañero*. This is the case among Mexicans, Salvadorans, Cubans, and Puerto Ricans and it is increasingly being adopted by other Latino groups. The Latino celebration of the 15th birthday of girls is similar to debutante and sweet 16 celebrations, except that it has additional religious and social connotations. The *quinceañera* dresses up in a formal white, pink, or pastel-colored gown and a tiara for a party in her honor. In many cases the party is preceded by a ceremony in church where the family gives thanks for the gift of having a daughter and where the girl accepts the responsibilities associated with her newly attained adult status. *Quinceañera* ceremonies and parties, like the weddings that they resemble, are as expensive and as extravagant as the families can afford. The food for the party used to be homemade festive foods like tamales, chicken in *mole*, roast goat or *pozole* (hominy stew) in the case of Mexicans, and roast pork and *pasteles* (plantain and root vegetable tamales) in the case of Puerto Ricans. Today *quinceañera* parties are likely to be catered and the food served can be the usual cold or hot buffet foods, sometimes combined with *antojitos* (Mexican snacks) or with vaguely Latino-inspired entrees. One innovation in the way in which *quinceañera* parties are celebrated in the United States is the selection of a theme for the party. Themes like "the '60s," "Arabian nights," "Brazilian carnival,"

Quinceañera cake. © J. Susan Cole Stone.

and others determine the decoration of the salon, the attire of the guests, and the food served. *Quinceañera* party food is as likely to be Latino as any other kind.

At weddings it is customary to throw handfuls of uncooked rice at the couple as a symbol of prosperity and fertility. There is also a reception and a banquet that is usually catered and may or may not consist of Latino food. In some cases, particularly among Mexicans, there is a party after the reception that is called *tornaboda*. A *tornaboda* is a gathering of only the closest family and friends of the newlyweds that can take place past midnight after the reception is over or during the next day. If the *tornaboda* is celebrated past midnight, the guests are served *antojitos* and *menudo* or *pozole*. If it is celebrated the next day, they are served an elaborate breakfast or brunch. In either case, sharing a late night meal or breakfast with the closest friends and family members gives the couple the opportunity to relax and talk about the wedding before leaving for their honeymoon.

Christmastime celebrations are the biggest and most joyful in the Latino calendar. Varied and elaborate, the foods served during this period constitute a collection of dishes that are used for other celebrations during the year. In Mexican and Mexican American culture, the Christmas season begins on December 16 with the celebration of nine nights of *posadas* that reenact Mary and Joseph's search for shelter when traveling to Bethlehem. Each night a different house is chosen by family and neighbors to host a dinner for the whole group. The celebration includes a *piñata* for the kids and traditional Christmas songs. Many Puerto Ricans in the United States keep the tradition of *parrandas*, in which friends form a musical ensemble with traditional Puerto Rican instruments and visit each other to sing Puerto Rican Christmas songs and to make merry with food and drink. In general, Christmas Eve rather than Christmas day is when the main celebration takes place. In many cases Christmas dinner is served late on Christmas Eve after attending mass, and at midnight the baby Jesus is put in the cradle of the nativity scene.

The Christmas table is set with festive and elaborate dishes, including appetizers, desserts, and drinks. Certain dishes are synonymous with Christmas and no celebration is complete without them. The central dishes are a great variety of regional tamales and roast pork or stuffed turkey. For those that do not have the time or the skill to cook traditional festive dishes, full Christmas meals and individual dishes are sold ready to cook or ready to serve. In Miami Cubans can buy a complete ready-to-serve meal of roast pork, white rice, black beans, yuca with garlic *mojo,* and flan. Mexicans and Central Americans can place their order for tamales well in advance and Puerto Ricans do the same with their roast pork, *pasteles,* and *morcillas* (blood sausage). While tamales are eaten year-round, Christmas tamales tend to have

Roasted pork. Courtesy of Nadine Pagán.

more ingredients and more complex flavoring. The tamales preferred by Guatemalans for Christmas are *tamales colorados* that are stuffed with pork, olives, and raisins in a red sauce made with tomatoes, chiles, and ground sesame and pumpkin seeds. They also favor *tamales negros*, made with a dark sauce of ground seeds, chiles, and chocolate. Nicaraguans and Hondurans opt for the large *nacatamal* that has a large number of filling ingredients both enclosed in and kneaded into the dough. Puerto Ricans and Dominicans must have *pasteles* made with a dough of ground plantains, green bananas, and root vegetables, and a pork filling. For Venezuelans and Colombians the tamal of choice is the *hallacas* that are stuffed with a rich pork, chicken, and beef stew. Mexicans have dozens of regional tamales to choose from, made with different meats in all kinds of salsas, *moles*, and *pipianes*. Sweet dessert tamales are also enjoyed during the holidays. Those who prepare their own tamales at home often transform the occasion into a party in itself, which is called a *tamalada*. Making tamales is labor-intensive because it requires the preparation of dough, filling, and sauce, and the individual assembly and wrapping of each tamal. When making tamales people prefer to make large quantities and enlist the help of friends and family, distributing the work assembly-line style. The *tamalada* is like a Christmas preview that creates the atmosphere of sharing and togetherness.

Red Tamales (Mexican)

For the filling:

1 pound boneless pork butt
  or shoulder, cut in large
  pieces
4 cloves garlic
1 small onion, quartered

5 peppercorns
1 bay leaf
3 ancho chiles
1/2 tsp salt
1 TBSP olive oil

For the *masa* (dough):

2 cups instant corn *masa*
  flour such as *Masa Harina*
  or *Maseca*
1 tsp baking powder
1 tsp salt

1 1/2 cup warm broth
1/3 cup lard, butter, or vegetable shortening, in any
  combination
12 dried corn husks

To make the filling, put the pork, onion, two cloves garlic, peppercorns, and salt in a saucepan with 2 cups of water, or enough to cover. Bring it to a boil and simmer until tender, about 45 minutes. When cool, remove the meat from the saucepan and shred it. Strain and reserve the resulting stock. Split open the chiles, discarding the seeds and veins. In a heavy skillet over medium heat, roast the chiles for a few seconds on both sides until blistered. Break them into small pieces and soak in hot water for 30 minutes. Grind in a mortar and pestle or blender with two cloves garlic, adding water as necessary to form a paste. Heat the olive oil in a skillet and fry the chile puree for 3 minutes, stirring constantly. Add a little water if necessary to prevent the sauce from burning. Add the shredded meat and cook for 3 more minutes.

Make the *masa* only after making the filling. In a mixing bowl combine the instant corn *masa* flour, baking powder, salt, and 1 1/2 cups broth left over from making the filling. In the bowl of an electric mixer beat the butter, lard, or shortening until fluffy. Add the flour and broth batter a third at a time, beating well after each addition. When all the batter has been incorporated, beat on high speed for at least 5 minutes or until the batter is fluffy and has a spreadable consistency. Add more broth or water if necessary.

Soak the dried corn husks in very hot water for 15 minutes or until pliable. Tear some of the husks to form narrow strips to tie the tamales. Place a husk on the working surface with the narrow end toward you. Spread 1/2 cup *masa* across the husk, from the middle up to 1/4 inch from the top edge and all the way left and right. Place 3 tablespoons of the pork filling in the

(*continued*)

middle and fold in both sides of the husk to overlap. Fold the bottom end up to meet the top, and tie around the middle using a husk strip. Steam the tamales standing up vertically for 1 hour over high heat.

The Christmas roast pork can be anything from a well-seasoned fresh ham cooked in the oven to a whole pig roasted in a bakery oven or in the outdoors roasting box known as *caja china*. Turkeys and other birds are marinated with garlic and herbs and stuffed with sweet and savory fillings. The Mexican *pavo de Navidad* is stuffed with milk-soaked bread rolls, onions, celery, apples, prunes, and nuts. Mexicans also mix sweet and savory flavors in Christmas salads that combine fruits and vegetables like jícama (crisp root vegetable), oranges, beets, and peanuts with honey, oil, and vinegar dressing. Salted codfish stews are another favorite holiday dish among Mexican Americans, and in New Mexico the meat and hominy stew called *pozole* is a Christmas tradition. Salvadorans might choose to serve their festive *gallo en chicha*, a rooster stewed in a fermented corn and fruit drink or in beer. Bolivians also have a traditional chicken stew for Christmas, called *picana de Navidad*, that includes vegetables like green peas, fresh maize, potatoes, carrots, tomatoes, and celery. A Brazilian specialty prepared during the holidays is the savory maize torte filled with vegetables and chicken or seafood called *cuscuz paulista*. The thick stews known as *sancocho* are a part of Dominican, Colombian, and Panamanian holiday tables.

Rice with pigeon peas decorated for Christmas with roasted sweet peppers. Courtesy of Nadine Pagán.

Pernil de Cerdo (Caribbean Roasted Pork Leg)

1 9-pound bone-in shank-
  end fresh ham
OR
1 8-pound bone-in pork
  shoulder (picnic roast)
6 TBSP salt

8 garlic cloves
1/2 TBSP dry oregano
1/2 TBSP freshly ground
  pepper
2 TBSP olive oil

In a mortar and pestle or food processor, grind all the seasoning ingredients to form a paste. Wash and dry the roast. With a sharp knife, lift the skin of the roast without breaking it. Make several incisions on the meat and spread the seasoning all over the meat and skin, inserting some into the incisions. Put the skin back into place. Wrap the roast well and refrigerate overnight. Take the roast out of the refrigerator 2 hours before roasting and preheat the oven to 350°. Place the roast on a deep roasting pan, skin side up, and cover with aluminum foil. Roast 30 minutes per pound, about 4–5 hours. The internal temperature in the thickest part should be 155°. When the roast is almost done, remove the aluminum foil and raise the oven temperature to 375° to crisp and brown the skin. Remove from the oven and let rest for 30 minutes before serving. Leftover roast slices can be used to make *Cubano* sandwiches.

Sancocho (Meat and Root Vegetable Stew)

1 whole skinless chicken,
  cut up, or 3 pounds beef
  or pork with bones
2 TBSP olive oil
2 small onions, chopped
4 garlic cloves, minced
2 bay leaves
1 Italian frying pepper or
  green bell pepper,
  chopped
1/2 pound fresh or frozen
  yuca
3/4 pound calabaza pumpkin,
  cut into large pieces

1/2 pound potatoes cut into
  2 inch cubes
1/2 pound yautía, ñame, or
  celery root, peeled and cut
  into 2 inch cubes
3 carrots, cut into 1 1/2
  inch pieces
2 ears corn, cut into 2 inch
  pieces
1 green plantain, peeled and
  sliced 1/2 inch thick
Salt and pepper to taste
1/4 cup cilantro, roughly
  chopped

(continued)

In a large stock pot or soup kettle heat the oil and sauté the onions, garlic, and pepper with the bay leaf until soft. Add the chicken pieces and cook until browned on all sides. Add about 10 cups of water and bring to a boil. Skim off the foam from the top and add all the remaining ingredients except for the cilantro. Cover the pot and simmer gently for 1 hour or until the chicken is cooked and the vegetables are tender. The pumpkin will have disintegrated and thickened the *sancocho*. Adjust the seasonings and stir in the cilantro.

Christmas is also a time for special sweets. In New Mexico and Arizona, Mexican American families enjoy *sopaipillas*, a flat dough that puffs up when deep-fried and that is served with honey. A similar treat prepared by many Latinos is *buñuelos*, which are fried balls of a butter- and egg-rich dough served in syrup. Along the same lines there is *torrejas*, pieces of white bread dipped in eggs, fried, and soaked in syrup. Many kinds of sweet breads are made or bought for the holidays, including panettones and fruitcakes that are South American favorites. Cuban Americans, Puerto Ricans, and many other Latinos also look for Christmas treats imported from Spain like *turrón* (almond nougat) and marzipan. Puerto Rican Christmas would not be complete without large plates of *arroz con dulce*, a thick rice pudding made with coconut milk and cinnamon. A festive dessert that is sought after during all holidays is *pastel tres leches* (three milk cake). This creamy milk-soaked cake is very popular all over Latin America and has become a favorite pan-Latino dessert.

Pastel Tres Leches (Three Milk Cake)

For the cake:

1 cup unbleached all-purpose flour	3/4 cup sugar
1/2 tsp baking powder	5 egg yolks
1/4 tsp salt	5 egg whites
5 TBSP butter	1/2 cup milk
	1 tsp vanilla extract

For the milks:

1 14-ounce can sweetened condensed milk	1 cup evaporated milk
	1 cup fresh whole milk

For the frosting:

1 cup heavy cream	1/4 cup sugar

Preheat the oven to 350°. Butter the bottom and sides of a 9-inch round cake pan. In a small bowl mix together the flour, salt, and baking powder. In a large mixing bowl use an electric mixer to beat the butter and sugar until light and creamy. Beat in the egg yolks, one at a time. Slowly mix in the flour mixture. Add the milk and vanilla and beat until well-mixed. In a separate bowl, beat the egg whites until stiff peaks form. Carefully fold the egg whites into the batter using a spatula. Pour the batter into the pan and bake for 25 minutes or until a toothpick inserted in the middle comes out clean. Let the cake cool in the pan for 10 minutes. Unmold the cake and let it cool on a rack. When totally cooled, place the cake on a wide-rimmed plate and pierce it all over with a fork.

Mix the three milks and pour them slowly and evenly over the cake, allowing it to absorb before adding more. Cover the cake with plastic wrap and refrigerate for at least 2 hours. Just before serving the cake, whip the heavy cream and sugar together until stiff peaks form. Spread the frosting over the cake and serve.

Latinos have many special drinks for the holidays beyond champagne, sparkling wines, beer, and rum. For the holidays Andean Americans celebrate with *chicha de jora*, a fermented maize drink. Chileans and other South American in the United States prepare a drink called *cola de mono* with *pisco* or any other *aguardiente* (eau-de-vie or brandy), condensed milk, and coffee spiced with cloves, vanilla, and cinnamon. Many Latinos from South America serve *clericó* (white sangría), and Mexican Americans and Central American immigrants have their own versions of eggnog called *rompope*. A Puerto Rican Christmas drink is *coquito*, made with rum and sweetened coconut cream.

Coquito (Puerto Rican Coconut and Rum Christmas Drink)

3 cinnamon sticks	1 1/2 cup evaporated milk
1 cup water	1–1 1/2 cup white rum
1 15-ounce can sweetened coconut cream	

Bring the water and cinnamon sticks to a boil. Turn off the heat, cover, and let cool. In a blender combine the cinnamon water (without the cinnamon

(continued)

sticks), coconut cream, evaporated milk, and rum and mix for 1 full minute on high speed. Refrigerate until very cold and shake well before serving. Serve in shot glasses.

The Christmas season continues with the celebration of New Year's Eve. At this time many Latinos continue a Spanish tradition of eating 12 grapes at midnight ideally in synchronicity with the 12 chimes of the clock. The grapes are put into a champagne glass, and the toast with champagne or with *cava* (Spanish sparkling wine) is supposed to happen only after the grapes are eaten. The ritual to attract good luck for the 12 months of the New Year is performed with a sense of humor, given the difficulties of eating 12 grapes so quickly.

On January 6 the holiday table is set up again for the celebration of the Epiphany, or Three Kings Day, commemorating the arrival of the three wise men to pay their respects to the baby Jesus in Bethlehem. Traditionally children receive gifts on this date, although the popularity of Santa Claus both in the United States and in Latin America has eclipsed this practice. Puerto Rican kids on the island and in the United States put grass in a shoebox to feed the camels of the three kings and in the morning they find that the grass has been substituted with a gift. Mexican children look forward to the *rosca de reyes*, a ring-shaped spiced sweet bread with candied fruit that contains at least one heat-resistant plastic doll hidden inside. The shape of the bread represents the crown of the kings and the hidden doll represents the baby Jesus that the kings were trying to locate. The person that finds the doll in his or her piece of bread becomes king or queen for the day and is also required to host a party or at least buy the tamales for the celebration of Candlemas. Sometimes the bread contains two dolls: one baby and one king and the person that finds the king has to serve the one that finds the baby for the rest of the party. Candlemas on February 2 is the last celebration in the Christmas holiday season, and it commemorates the purification of the Virgin 40 days after giving birth.

In Latin America, carnival is a pre-Lenten festival that ends on Ash Wednesday when the abstinence period begins. Many people do not fast at all while others fast only on Fridays or just abstain from or control any favorite activity instead of fasting. The origin of the excess of food, drink, and sensuality displayed during carnival is traced back to a time when people were expected to abstain or control all pleasures of the flesh like eating, drinking, dancing, and sex during the Lenten period. The festivities with street dancing in colorful and revealing clothes have outlived the practice of abstinence that was supposed to follow, and many people prepare their floats and outfits for this celebration during the whole year. Carnival in Latin America and the Caribbean has always been associated with the suspension or reversal of social hierarchies and with the relaxation of rules. In the United States, Latino carnivals are more like international cultural or tourist exhibitions. Corporate sponsorship, media coverage, and more than 1 million participants from different countries distinguish the largest and most successful Latino carnival: the Miami carnival that culminates with the *Calle Ocho* street festival in Little Havana. This event started as a Cuban American festival that grew and changed to accommodate the growing diversity of the Latino population of Miami and that eventually became a huge event dubbed "the largest party in the Hispanic market" by its organizers. The festival features music, dancing, sports competitions, and a beauty contest as well as a banquet, a cooking contest, and plenty of Latino and international foods. Roast meats like pork and goat, *arepas* (maize griddle cakes), *ceviche* (citrus-marinated raw fish pieces), and many other foods are sold by street vendors. While the Miami carnival can still be seen as a Latino event in spite of its size and corporate participation, other so-called Latino carnivals have little or no community base. One example is the Brazil Carnaval celebrated in Hollywood Park Casino in Los Angeles, an event attended almost exclusively by non-Brazilians wearing regular nightclub attire. Brazilian food like *feijoada* (black bean stew with a variety of meats) is a part of a cultural spectacle set up for a passive audience that consumes a stereotypical Brazilianness.[3]

When Easter arrives Mexican Americans in the Southwest celebrate with confetti-filled eggs called *cascarones*. Traditionally people save eggshells for weeks, cleaning and drying them. The eggs are dyed, decorated, and filled with colorful confetti. The shell opening is closed with glued-on colored tissue paper. On Easter and other celebrations the eggs are cracked on people's heads as a way of spreading good luck and cheer. *Cascarones* can be store-bought and are also sold on the streets on major holidays.

Each Latin American country and town has its own patron saint and there are annual feasts in their honor. In the United States, Latinos have continued the celebrations of the patron saint of their or their family's hometown. Patron saint day festivities have a religious origin, but in the case of diasporic peoples, they are better understood as community-building events. Patron saint feasts become celebrations of the different nationalities and of establishing their continuity outside of their respective countries. There are organizations devoted to the cult of the patron saint that organize the annual festivities. The patron saint feast usually involves a mass and a procession with the image of the saint. Around these events there are plenty of traditional foods sold on the street as well as in private banquets.

Mexicans celebrate the feast of the Virgin of Guadalupe on December 12. Foods available during the days of celebration include festive foods like *pozole* and *menudo*, sweets made with *piloncillo* (raw cane sugar) and pumpkin, and street foods like tacos, *aguas frescas* (fresh-fruit beverages), and corn on the cob dressed with mayonnaise and chile. Part of this celebration is the *carrera de la antorcha guadalupana* (Guadalupe Torch Run), in which runners leave from the Basilica of the Virgin of Guadalupe in México City in October and pass through many Mexican and U.S. states to arrive in New York City in time for the celebration of the patroness' day. The torch run is a way of uniting Mexicans on both sides of the border and of advocating the rights of undocumented immigrants. Local patron saints also have transnational celebrations, as in the case of the Feast of Father Jesus, celebrated in a coordinated fashion in New York and in Ticuani, a southern Mexican town in the Mixteca region. Ticuani people on both sides of the border come together over these festivals and negotiate their shared identity as expressed by shared cultural practices, including food, rather than by where they live.[4]

The celebration of the patron saint of towns rather than countries is especially important for Latinos that belong to less visible communities like indigenous Central Americans. In Los Angeles the *Feria de San Miguel* (Feast of Saint Michael) is celebrated on September 29 by Kanjobal Mayas from the town of San Miguel de Ixtatán in western Guatemala. The feast reproduces all the details of the festivities of their hometown.[5] Celebrations with foods like freshly made tortillas, *frijoles volteados* (thick fried bean puree), *pepián* (meat in ground pumpkin seed sauce), and *pacaya* (palm blossom) are instrumental in the ongoing process of creating a common cultural identity and a space for all Central American in the United States.

Puerto Ricans celebrate the day of their patron Saint John the Baptist on June 24, which coincides with the summer solstice. An important part of this festivity is walking backward into the ocean at midnight for good luck. Puerto Ricans also celebrate the feast of their patroness Our Lady of Divine Providence on November 19, purposefully coinciding with the day on which Christopher Columbus arrived on the island. Since Puerto Ricans do not have a national independence day, this and events like the National Puerto Rican Day Parade in New York City allow for the celebration of Puertoricanness without reference to a nation state. In Puerto Rican festivities in the United States, as well as on the island, foods like *arroz con gandules* (rice with pigeon peas), *pasteles*, *bacalaítos* (codfish fritters), and *alcapurrias* (green banana and yautía—underground plant stem—fritters with meat filling) help to create the party atmosphere. For Cuban Americans, the celebration of the feast of their patroness Our Lady of Charity every September 8 is more solemn because they relate it to the political situation of Cuba. The Virgin is seen as the protector of Cubans that have left the island and as a force that will bring a change of government in Cuba.

Another Latin American patron saint with a strong following in the United States is *Señor de los Milagros* (Our Lord of the Miracles), patron saint of Lima, Perú. The Vatican and the Archbishop of Lima decided to establish October 15 as the day of the Feast of *Señor de los Milagros,* now considered as patron saint of both resident and immigrant Peruvians. Everywhere that there is a large concentration of Peruvian immigrants there is an association devoted to the celebration of this feast. Aside from the usual mass and procession, private banquets are likely to include some sort of *pachamanca,* which is an Andean dish of meat, potatoes, and other vegetables cooked over heated stones covered with grass and earth. Other festive foods are also part of the festivities but *Señor de los Milagros* is also celebrated with a specific sweet called *turrón de doña Pepa* (Mrs. Pepa's nougat). This very elaborate sweet is a heavy, layered torte. Thin logs made with aniseed-flavored pastry are placed side by side forming flat layers that are filled and bound together with a syrup made with *chancaca* (raw cane sugar) flavored with fruits and spiced with cinnamon and cloves. The top is decorated with tiny candies of different shapes and colors. This nougat can be made at home but it is readily available from food importers.

Latin American national holidays are celebrated by Latinos with festivals and parades. The National Puerto Rican Day Parade in New York is the oldest and largest Latino parade, although similar parades are organized by all Latino groups. The parades feature colorful floats that are often sponsored by food companies like Goya. Traditional foods of the corresponding nationality are sold on the streets alongside the parades. There are also street festivals celebrating the independence day of Latin American countries. For Mexican independence day (September 16), Mexican Americans like preparing *chiles en nogada* (*poblano* chiles stuffed with meat and covered with ground walnut sauce and pomegranate seeds) and foods that feature the colors of the Mexican flag, like a platter of green, white, and red rice. The green rice is colored with cilantro, *poblano* chiles, and *tomatillos* (green husk tomatoes), while the red one gets its color from tomatoes. Perhaps the most popular Latino celebration is the Mexican Cinco de Mayo, which commemorates the defeat of the French army by Mexican forces in Puebla in 1862. This is a minor regional celebration in México that in the United States has become a major day for the celebration and commercialization of Mexican food and culture.

FASTING

The Catholic calendar imposes the abstention from eating meat during the 40 days of Lent. Over the centuries special meatless dishes were developed to gratify the taste buds without breaking the fast. Today the majority of Latin Americans and Latinos do not fast or fast only on selected days like Good Friday. Nevertheless, Lenten dishes are still prepared by many because they give a sense of the season and because they are delicious. Many Lenten dishes come from the Spanish and Portuguese traditions and are based on *bacalao* (salted codfish) and chickpeas. Other dishes were devised to make use of the bounty of the seas and of the seasonal vegetables of early spring.

During Lent, many Mexicans in the United States prepare traditional fish and shellfish dishes like seafood stews and turnovers filled with *bacalao* or young shark. Other Lenten dishes are poblano chiles stuffed with cheese and *tamal de Judas* made with maize, beans, or peas and *piloncillo* (raw cane sugar). A specialty from Oaxaca is *empanadas de Corpus Christi*, which are flaky turnovers filled with fruit preserves or pastry cream. Other sweet dishes favored during this season are rice pudding and *capirotadas* (bread pudding flavored with syrup made with *piloncillo,* cinnamon, cloves, and aniseed).

For Lent, Caribbean Americans eat fresh fish and seafood and a variety of salted codfish dishes including stews, salads, and croquettes. A Basque specialty that is a Caribbean favorite is *bacalao a la vizcaína.* For this dish the soaked codfish is lightly stewed with olive oil, tomatoes, onions, garlic, olives, and capers, and served with boiled potatoes. The traditional Lenten dish for Puerto Ricans is *serenata de bacalao,* a light salad of boiled and flaked codfish dressed with olive oil, onion, tomatoes, and avocado. It is served with boiled vegetables like yautía, green bananas, ripe plantains, yuca, and *calabaza* pumpkin. A classic Dominican Lenten dish is *habichuelas con dulce,* which is a sweetened red bean puree thinned with milk or coconut milk. It is served garnished with raisins, sweet potato, and cookies.

Central Americans in the United States also focus on fresh and dry fish during the Lenten period. Salvadorans traditionally serve dry fish in *tortas de pescado.* To make this dish, dry fish is soaked, enveloped in egg batter or in maize *masa* (nixtamalized dough), and fried. The fried fish is then stewed in a tomato, onion, and chile sauce and served with chickpeas and potatoes. Fruits like mangoes and *jocotes* poached in raw cane sugar syrup are another Salvadoran Lenten staple. Guatemalans have a specialty dish called *pacaya en huevo* that is usually served during this season. *Pacayas* are the blossom of a date palm tree, which is covered in egg batter and fried. Central Americans, like most Latinos, prepare traditional Spanish codfish dishes during Lent.

Latinos with South American backgrounds also enjoy *bacalao,* fresh fish, and shellfish preparations for Lent. Many elaborate fish and vegetable soups are synonymous with this season like the Ecuadorian *fanesca,* which is traditionally served on Holy Thursday and makes full use of spring produce. During Lent Ecuadorian shops in the United States announce that they have all the ingredients necessary to make *fanesca* and many restaurants make it a special item on their menu. *Fanesca* is a very thick soup that combines different kinds of bean with maize kernels, rice, peas, green beans, and peanuts with pureed zucchini and squashes. Milk, cheese, and codfish are added to the thick mixture and the soup is served with a variety of garnishes like hard-boiled egg slices, fried ripe plantains, red bell pepper strips, and *empanadas de viento* (small cheese turnovers). Another Lenten specialty is the Bolivian *quesumacha*, a dish of potatoes in a sauce made with peas, fava beans, milk, onions, tomatoes, and grated fresh cheese. South American Lenten dishes also include cooked vegetable salads that constitute meals in themselves. These salads contain ingredients like potatoes, fava beans, fresh maize, peas, lupini beans, onion, tomato, and avocado and are dressed with vinaigrette. Mayonnaise salads with tuna or vegetables like potatoes and carrots are also popular.

FEEDING THE SPIRITUAL WORLD

In Latin America the Catholic practices imposed by the Spanish and Portuguese were refashioned through indigenous and African religions, creating new and distinct ways of conceiving divinity and the afterlife. Food plays an important role in the way in which Latin American cultures relate to the spiritual world, as can be seen in the celebration of the Day of the Dead and in the practice of religions like *santería* and *candomblé*. Whereas many Latinos engage in these practices for their cultural rather than their religious value, they still show that food feeds more than the material body.

In the regular Catholic calendar November 1 and 2 are All Saints Day and All Souls Day, respectively. All over the world Catholics take time to remember their dead loved ones at this time. When the Spanish imposed Catholic rituals, these holidays became an outlet for preexisting indigenous festivals that honored the ancestors. Whereas All Souls Day is a minor holiday for most Latin Americans, the survival and transformation of indigenous festivals gives the Mexican, Guatemalan, and Ecuadorian celebrations of this holiday a character of their own. The celebration of *Día de Muertos* in México varies by region but it generally involves visiting the cemeteries and bringing food to feed dead family members that, according to the tradition, are allowed to return to the earth as spirits once a year. It also involves the preparation of altars with pictures of the dead, candles, marigolds, and foods and other items that the dead person liked. Visits to the cemetery are not always practical for Mexican Americans but the creation of altars continues and has become an art form. The preparation of special foods also continues. Sugar skulls with colorful decorations and bearing the name of dead and alive family and friends are eaten as a way of accepting or even challenging death. Egg-rich breads spiced with aniseed (*pan de muerto*), tamales, and any food that dead family members used to enjoy are also an integral part of the celebration.

Mexican Day of the Dead altar, New York. Photo by Zilkia Janer.

Guatemalans also celebrate the Day of the Dead by visiting the cemetery and adorning the graves with marigolds. A highlight of the holiday in Guatemala is the flying of colorful giant kites made of tissue paper and bamboo. The kites symbolically help the dead communicate with the living. *Fiambre* is a dish reserved exclusively for this celebration. It is a chilled salad composed of dozens of artfully arranged ingredients that is as colorful as the giant kites. The ingredients for *fiambre* are pickled vegetables like beets, peas, mushrooms, cabbage, lettuce, green beans, carrots, asparagus, Brussels sprouts, *pacaya*, chayote squash, and cauliflower, as well as fresh and cured meats like chicken, ham, and many different kinds of sausages. The ingredients are dressed with vinegar, ginger, mustard, capers, and parsley and they are carefully arranged or layered. The dish is garnished with hard-boiled eggs, capers, red chiles, beets, olives, and cheese. Guatemalans in the United States make their own *fiambre* at home or buy it from businesses that serve scaled-down versions.

Ecuadorian Americans celebrate the *Día de los Difuntos* (Day of the Dead) with baby-shaped breads called *guaguas de pan*. The light and sweet bread dolls are decorated with raisins and sugar icing to create faces and clothes and they might also have a jam filling. They are eaten with a glass of hot *colada morada*, a thick dark drink made with purple cornmeal and fruits. The tradition of eating these foods comes from Andean cultures that consider preparing and consuming certain foods and drinks as prayer or as a medium to communicate with dead ancestors. It is also compatible with the Catholic ritual of transubstantiation and communion, in which bread and red wine are

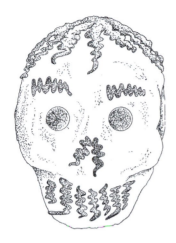

Sugar skull. © J. Susan Cole Stone.

transformed into the body and blood of Christ. Consuming *guaguas de pan* and *chicha* is a symbolic way of communion with dead family members.

Caribbean and Brazilian Americans who practice Yoruba-derived religions like *santería* and *candomblé* incorporate foods into their rituals in a variety of ways. Yoruba religion was brought by African slaves to the Americas, where it was transformed into contemporary *santería* in the Caribbean and *candomblé* in Brazil. *Santería* also incorporates elements from Roman Catholicism and from Spiritism or Kardecism. Cubans and Puerto Ricans brought *santería* to Miami, New York, and other cities, where it has continued to grow and adapt, becoming an important form of Latino popular religiosity. Practitioners of *santería* engage in the communication with deities or *santos* known as *orishas*. Each *orisha* has influence over specific aspects of human life and is related to one or more Catholic saints. They are also thought to have specific food preferences that their devotees offer to them routinely to nourish their relationship, or on specific occasions to ask for protection or to give thanks for good fortune. The offering can be as simple as a fruit or as elaborate as a feast in honor of the *orisha*. Yemayá, for example, is the patron saint of motherhood and is identified with Our Lady of Regla. Common food offerings for her are banana chips, black-eyed peas, cane molasses, and watermelon. Obatalá is the most powerful *orisha* and is considered the father of humanity. He is associated with Our Lady of Ransom and with the color white, which represents purity. His food preferences include many white foods like meringues, coconuts, cocoa butter, and rice pudding. Changó represents fire and thunder, and he is the patron saint of revenge upon enemies. He is related to Saint Barbara, Saint Mark, and Saint Expeditus, among others. The foods offered to Changó include apples, cornmeal, okra, red wine, bananas, and cactus fruits.[6] In some cases, devotees of a specific *orisha* abstain from their *orisha's* favorite food as a sign of respect. Animal sacrifice occurs occasionally and only following a strict set of rules. The sacrificed animal is most frequently a bird and in some cases it is cooked and eaten after being offered to the *orisha*. The bird is not consumed when the sacrifice is part of a ritual cleansing because its role is to absorb the negative energy that is expelled from the devotee and it must be discarded.[7] In Brazilian *candomblé*, *dendê* oil (palm oil) is used in rituals and in the preparation of votive foods. Many specialties from Bahia, where *candomblé* is widely practiced, are prepared with *dendê* oil, which gives a distinctive taste to dishes like *moqueca* stews, *acarajé* fritters, and *caruru* (okra stew).

In *santería*, pieces of the flesh of dry coconut are used in divination ceremonies through which the *orishas* communicate with followers, offering advice, answering questions, and warning about the future. Herbs and plants are used to make *omieros*, sacred waters made with the extract of dozens of different plants. *Omieros* are used in initiation ceremonies and in other rituals designed to attract love, good luck, or protection. Originally only wild plants from the fields and the forest were considered suitable, although now specialty stores called *botánicas* provide the needed plants. Ordained *santería* priests, called *santeros*, are experts on the curative powers of plants. *Santeros* are often consulted in cases of illness and they prescribe herbs as appropriate. It is considered that illness has both biological and spiritual dimensions and *santería* strives to address both. For this reason herbal remedies are seen as complementary to modern medicine and many people see both a *santero* and a doctor to treat their conditions. The benefits of indigenous herbal medicine are not only being recognized by the medical establishment, but also increasingly appropriated in the form of patents that turn traditional Latin American knowledge into corporate property.

NOTES

1. Mario Montaño, "Appropriation and Counterhegemony in South Texas: Food Slurs, Offal Meats, and Blood," in *Usable Pasts: Traditions and Group Expressions in North America*, ed. Tad Tuleja (Logan: Utah State University Press, 1997), p. 53.

2. Brett Williams, "Why Migrant Women Feed Their Husbands Tamales: Foodways as a Basis for a Revisionist View of Tejano Family Life," in *Ethnic and Regional Foodways in the United States: The Performance of Group Identity*, ed. Linda Keller Brown and Kay Mussell (Knoxville: University of Tennessee Press, 1984), p. 116.

3. Bernadete Beserra, "From Brazilians to Latinos? Racialization and Latinidad in the Making of Brazilian Carnival in Los Angeles," *Latino Studies* 3, no. 1 (2005): 68.

4. Robert C. Smith, *Mexican New York: Transnational Lives of New Immigrants* (Berkeley: University of California Press, 2006), p. 162.

5. Arturo Arias, "Central American-Americans? Re-mapping Latino/Latin American Subjectivities on Both Sides of the Great Divide (Social, Cultural Presence, Influences, of Central Americans in the United States)," *Explicación de Textos Literarios* 47, no. 17 (Winter–Summer 1999): 47–48.

6. Miguel A. de la Torre, *Santería: The Beliefs and Rituals of a Growing Religion in America* (Grand Rapids, Mich.: William B. Eerdmans, 2004), pp. 48–58, 121–125.

7. De la Torre, *Santería*, pp. 123–127.

7

Diet and Health

Latinos have a rich heritage of dietary and medicinal knowledge that includes Hippocratic-Galenic humoral medicine and Amerindian and African botanical medicine. These traditions are combined with modern nutritional science to form a flexible and idiosyncratic system. While few Latinos have an in-depth knowledge of any of these systems, many traditional dietary and medicinal guidelines are practiced as common sense alongside modern ones. Traditional Latin American diets used to give central stage to maize, beans, rice, and fresh fruits and vegetables, reserving the richer meat-based dishes for occasional comsumption. However, the lifestyle changes associated with urbanization in Latin America and with migration to the United States have resulted in increased health problems like obesity, diabetes, and hypertension in the Latino population. This situation has sparked a revalorization of traditional Latino approaches to diet and health.

HEALTH ISSUES

In 2005, the market research firm NPD group published a report on the food habits of Latinos. The study found that as Latinos adapt to life in the United States they adopt the prevalent eating habits in which convenient foods substitute for traditional ones. Eating out at fast-food restaurants and the consumption of carbonated soft drinks, chips, sandwiches, and preprepared foods increase while the intake of fruits, vegetables, and fresh foods cooked from scratch decreases.[1] Consequently the incidence of diet-related diseases like diabetes and hypertension is on the rise in the Latino population.

The incidence of poor health among Latinos is higher among migrant farm workers and day laborers, who do not earn enough money to secure enough basic food and often face hunger. Ironically, even though Latino farm workers produce the bulk of fruits and vegetables consumed in the United States, they depend on inexpensive high-fat fast foods.[2] They live in isolated labor camps often without cooking facilities, and they have little access to grocery stores and to health care. Immigrants in urban and suburban contexts face similar difficulties that affect their diet and health. A study of the eating habits of Mexican families from the state of Oaxaca in New Jersey found that migration had a negative impact on health.[3] Immigrant women explained the difficulties of continuing their Oaxacan eating habits in New Jersey and expressed fears of losing their traditional food and health knowledge. Without access to land, most urban Latinos cannot grow fresh fruits and vegetables, despite having the required skills. Because of poor economic conditions, those located in other areas also lack the time and resources to do that, increasingly making most Latino communities dependent on processed food. Low income and undocumented status prevent access to health care and to educational sources to learn how to make better choices in their new food environment. Even in cases of relative prosperity, the health of immigrants tends to suffer. The children of immigrants have a high obesity rate, particularly when their parents had suffered from food scarcity in the past. Among middle-class Latinos, the adoption of mainstream U.S. eating habits, and the more frequent consumption of rich traditional dishes that used to be reserved for special occasions, also results in weight gain and other health problems.

NUTRITIONAL VALUE OF LATINO FOODS

The high incidence of diet-related disease among Latinos has created the misconception that Latino food is unhealthy. However, since Latin American traditional diets did not cause such problems in the past, the cause of the rise of diabetes and hypertension among urban Latin Americans and among Latinos in the United States is better explained by socioeconomic factors like the modernization of food production in Latin America and the generally disadvantaged life conditions faced by Latinos in the United States.

Traditional Latino food culture has many of the characteristics that diet and health professionals consider ideal. Latino meals feature many different kinds of food, which helps to obtain a balanced nutrition. Dessert is not a part of all meals, which helps to control weight. Latinos also tend to make dinner time a special time to sit down and enjoy the company of family and friends rather than eating alone or on the go. Fresh meals made from scratch are highly valued and many Latinos have the skills necessary to produce them. All these positive aspects are on the decline but there are active efforts to keep them alive. Such efforts tend to focus more on information and marketing than on the socioeconomic conditions that make traditional eating patterns increasingly difficult. The Latino Nutrition Coalition recently published a Latino food pyramid that shows the public how traditional Latino foods fit in the food guide pyramid of the U.S. Department of Agriculture. The Latino food pyramid uses foods like maize, tortillas, potatoes, plantains, avocados, and papayas to illustrate how to compose a balanced Latino meal. Latino food companies for their part have been quick to provide low-fat and low-sodium versions of their products.

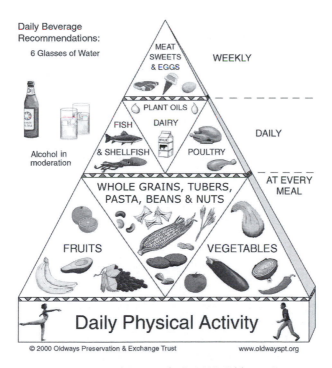

Latin American Food Pyramid. © 2000 Oldways Preservation and Exchange Trust. Used by permission.

Latino staple foods are highly nutritious and there is no reason to avoid them. Maize, a good source of carbohydrates, is low in fat. It also provides soluble fiber, protein, vitamins like B6, thiamin, niacin, and riboflavin, and minerals like magnesium, manganese, and selenium. Other starchy staples like potatoes, plantains, and yuca are very low in fat and are a good source of carbohydrates and fiber. Potatoes with their skin on are a good source of vitamin C, vitamin B6, potassium, and manganese. Plantains are an excellent source of antioxidant vitamins A and C, potassium, and vitamin B6. Research suggests that potassium helps lower blood pressure and prevents cardiac disease. Yuca is high in vitamin C and also provides important quantities of manganese, potassium, and folate. Beans, another staple of the Latino diet, are packed with protein that makes them ideal for a vegetarian diet. They are also high in soluble fiber, which helps reduce cholesterol levels. Beans are also an important source of vitamins B1 and B6 and folate, and minerals like manganese, potassium, and magnesium.

Nonstaple Latino foods are also packed with important nutrients. Chiles are an excellent source of vitamin C, and they are also rich in vitamins A and K. Vitamins C and A are antioxidants that help neutralize the effects of harmful free radicals. Chiles also contain capsaicin, the substance that gives them their characteristic heat and that is also a powerful decongestant. Avocados are high in fat but most of it is monounsaturated. The fruit's high fiber and monounsaturated fat content might help to control cholesterol levels. Avocados are also high in vitamin C, folate, and potassium. Summer squashes like zucchini provide vitamins C, A, K, and folate, as well as the minerals manganese and magnesium. Winter squashes like pumpkin are extremely high in vitamin A and also provide vitamin C, manganese, and potassium. Tomatoes are an excellent source of vitamin C and are also a good source of vitamin A, potassium, and manganese. They are high in lycopene, a substance that might have anticarcinogenic and antiatherogenic properties. Fruits that are frequently consumed by Latinos are also important sources of nutrition. Mango and papaya are excellent sources of vitamins A and C, and are rich in beta carotene.

HERBAL HOME REMEDIES

Rural and indigenous medicinal practices from Latin America form the core of folk healing practices that coexist with modern medicine among Latinos in the United States. In south Texas the *curandero* (healer) is a source of culturally sensitive health resources that treat common illnesses at the material, spiritual, and mental level.[4] Many Mexican Americans grow herbs at home or buy them at *yerberías* or *boticas* to use as first aid for common health problems.[5] Most Latinos are to a certain extent familiar with home remedies that use food, spices, and herbs as medicine. These are not used as a substitute for modern medicine but rather as a supplement. There are hundreds of herbal remedies, most of which are taken as an infusion. Common home remedies include aloe juice to aid digestion, chamomile, and *tilo* (linden) leaves tea for relaxation, star anise tea for gases and indigestion, cat's claw tea as an anti-inflammatory, *linaza* (flaxseed) as a laxative, and many others. Many of these infusions are now widely available in branded packages, and there are also books and Web sites that discuss the uses of herbs to improve health. As modern science catches up with the medicinal properties of herbs traditionally used in Latin America, multinational companies are aggressively engaged in biopiracy and acquiring patents rights to them. This means that indigenous communities are losing ownership rights to the biomedical knowledge they have produced over centuries.

NOTES

1. "Hispanics Readily Adopt American Eating Habits," *Consumeraffairs.com*, December 26, 2005, http://www.consumeraffairs.com/news04/2005/npd_hispanic_eating.html.

2. Tracie White, "Farmworkers' Dilemma: Not Eating What They Grow," *Stanford Report*, February 15, 2006.

3. Anne C. Bellows, "Oaxacan Women in New Jersey and Mexico: Family Health in the Context of Migration and Changing Food Environments" (paper presented at the 20th Joint Annual Meeting of the Agriculture, Food and Human Values Society and the Association for the Study of Food and Society, Victoria, B.C., Canada, June 2006).

4. Robert Trotter, *Curanderismo: Mexican American Folk Healing* (Athens: University of Georgia Press, 1981), p. 73.

5. Trotter, *Curanderismo*, pp. 51–56.

Glossary

Acarajé Brazilian black-eyed peas fritters.

Acelgas Swiss chard.

Achiote annatto; red seeds used to add flavor and color to food.

Adobo dry or wet seasoning mix used to prepare meats; for Caribbean Latinos, it is generally a mix of ground garlic, black pepper, salt, oregano, and vinegar; for Mexican Americans, it is a cooking tomato sauce seasoned with vinegar and spices.

Aguas frescas Mexican fresh-fruit drinks; popular flavors include tamarind, *jamaica* (hibiscus flower), cantaloupe, watermelon, and *horchata* (rice and cinnamon).

Ají chiles in South America and the Caribbean; also refers to hot sauces and dishes.

Ajiaco for Colombians, it is a chicken, maize, and potato stew; for Cubans, it is a heartier stew that combines chicken, pork, beef, and dried beef with plantains, pumpkin, maize, and different kinds of root vegetables.

Ajíes dulces sweet chiles that have a fragrance and taste similar to Habanero chiles with little or no heat; they are essential in Caribbean cuisines.

Ajilimójili Puerto Rican condiment made with garlic and *ajíes dulces* (sweet chiles).

Alcapurria Puerto Rican fritters made with a dough of ground green bananas, plantains, yautía, or yuca, and a savory ground meat or seafood filling.

Alfajores South American round cookies sandwiched with *dulce de leche* (caramelized milk) and covered with chocolate or powdered sugar.

Alguashte pumpkin-seed flour used in Central American cooking.

Anchos dried chiles used to make salsas and *moles.*

Anticuchos   grilled skewered meat from the Andean region; made with cow heart or any other type of meat, and the meat can be marinated with vinegar, garlic, and *ajíes* (hot chiles).

Antojitos   Mexican snacks or appetizers.

Arañitas   Puerto Rican fritter made with loosely gathered strands of grated green plantain.

Arepas   Colombian and Venezuelan griddle breads made with maize flour or ground fresh maize.

Arroz con leche   milky rice pudding flavored with cinnamon.

Arroz con pollo   chicken with rice.

Arroz moro   Dominican rice with beans and vegetables.

Asopao   Caribbean rice stews with chicken or seafood.

Atole   maize-based beverage.

Bacalaítos   Puerto Rican salted codfish fritters.

Bacalao   salted codfish.

Baleadas   Honduran tortillas filled with beans, cheese, and cream.

Bandeja paisa   Colombian "peasant platter," composed of rice, red beans, grilled meat, *chorizo* (sausage), *chicharrón* (fried pork rind), *arepa* (maize griddle bread), fried egg, and sliced avocado.

Barbacoa   pit roasting or barbecue.

Batidos   fruit milkshakes, also known as *licuados* or *batidas*.

Bistec   beefsteak.

Bodegas   corner stores in Latino neighborhoods.

Boliche   Cuban beef roast stuffed with *chorizo* (sausage).

Bolillos   bread rolls.

Boniato   sweet potato, also known as *batata* and *camote*.

Botánica   store that sells religious items for the practice of *santería* religion, including medicinal herbs.

Brigadeiros   Brazilian truffles made with sweetened condensed milk, butter, and cocoa powder.

Buñuelos   generic name for sweet fritters, of which there is a wide variety.

Cacahuazintle   variety of maize with large kernels that is preferred to make *pozole* (hominy stew) and *masa* (nixtamalized ground maize dough).

Cachaça   Brazilian alcoholic beverage made with distilled sugarcane juice.

Café con leche   coffee with steamed milk.

Café cubano   Cuban coffee, espresso with sugar.

Café de olla   Mexican coffee simmered with unrefined cane sugar, cinnamon, and anise seeds.

Caipirinha   Brazilian cocktail made with *cachaça,* lime, and sugar.

Caja china   "Chinese box" used to roast whole butterflied pigs.

Cal   slaked lime.

Calabaza   Caribbean pumpkin.

Caldero   heavy cast aluminum pots used in Puerto Rican cooking.

Canja   Brazilian chicken soup.

Capirotadas   Mexican dessert made with fried slices of bread served with syrup, dried fruits, nuts, and cheese.

Carambola   star fruit, also known as *maracuyá.*

Carimañola   Panamanian yuca fritters stuffed with meat.

Carnicería   butcher shop.

Caruru   Brazilian okra and shrimp stew.

Casabe   yuca bread.

Casamiento   Salvadoran rice with beans.

Cativías   (*catibías*) Dominican yuca and meat fritters.

Cau cau   Peruvian tripe stew.

Causa   Peruvian layered potato salad.

Cazuela   Mexican clay pot.

Ceviche   (*cebiche*) raw fish and shellfish marinated in citrus juice.

Chalupas   deep-fried maize *masa* (dough) containers or "boats" filled with meat and salsa.

Champurrado   Mexican chocolate and maize beverage; Guatemalan flat baking powder bread.

Chayote   small squash with crisp white flesh and a thick skin that can be either smooth or prickly, varying in color from white to light green, also known as *güisquil.*

Chicha   fermented beverage made of maize, yuca, or fruits.

Chicharrones   fried pork rinds.

Chifles   fried razor-thin plantain slices, also known as *mariquitas.*

Chilaquilas   Salvadoran fat tortillas that have been filled with cheese or meat, dipped in egg batter and fried.

Chilaquiles   Mexican casserole made with broken-up tortillas simmered in salsa.

Chimichurri   Argentinean parsley and garlic sauce; Dominican hamburger.

Chipá   Paraguayan yuca bread.

Chipilín   leafy vegetable used in Central American cuisine.

Chipotle   dried and smoked jalapeño chiles.

Chirimoya   custard apple.

Chirmol   Guatemalan salsa.

Choclo   fresh maize.

Chofán   Chinese fried rice, also known as *chaulafán* and *arroz chaufa*.

Cholados   Colombian sweet treat of layered ice, fruit syrup, fresh fruits, and condensed milk.

Choripan   Argentinean grilled **chorizo** (sausage) and French bread sandwich.

Chorizo   pork sausage seasoned with garlic and paprika.

Chuño   traditional Andean freeze-dried potatoes.

Chupe   soup or chowder.

Churrasco   Brazilian mixed grilled meats; Argentinean thick skirt steak.

Churros   fried wheat pastry strips.

Clericó   white sangría.

Cola de mono   Chilean drink made with *aguardiente* (brandy), coffee, and condensed milk.

Colada morada   Ecuadorian fruit and maize beverage.

Comal   griddle used to cook tortillas.

Completos   Chilean hot dogs.

Congris   Cuban rice with red beans, also known as *arroz congris* and *congrí*.

Coquito   Puerto Rican rum and coconut drink.

Coxinhas   Brazilian chopped chicken croquettes shaped to resemble a chicken leg.

Crema   Latin American–style cream, similar to *crème fraîche*.

Cuáker   Ecuadorian oatmeal beverage.

Cuba libre   cola, lime, and rum cocktail.

Cuchifritos   Puerto Rican snacks.

Curtido   Salvadoran shredded, pickled vegetables.

Cuscuz   Brazilian dish; *cuscuz nordestino* is a steamed cake made with flaked cornmeal and coconut milk; *cuscuz paulista* is a molded cake made with flaked cornmeal and a variety of meats and vegetables.

Cuy   guinea pig.

Dendê oil   bright orange palm oil used in Brazilian cooking.

Dulce de leche   caramelized milk, also known as *manjar*, *cajeta*, and *arequipe*.

Elote   fresh corn.

Empanadas   wheat, maize, or yuca turnovers with a great variety of sweet or savory fillings, also known as *pastelillos*, *pastelitos*, and *empanadillas*.

Enchilada   for Mexicans, it is a tortilla dipped in sauce, filled, and rolled or folded; for Central Americans, it is a tortilla fried flat with a filling on top.

Epazote   Mexican herb used for flavor and for medicinal properties like flatulence prevention.

Escabeche   generic name given to all kinds of pickled foods, also known as *encurtidos*.

Facturas   Argentinean pastries made with thin layers of puff pastry.

Fanesca   Ecuadorian Lenten soup.

Farofa   Brazilian toasted yuca flour.

Feijoada completa   Brazilian dish of black beans with a wide assortment of fresh and cured meats.

Fiambre   Guatemalan large composed salad prepared for Day of the Dead celebrations.

Flan   milk and egg custard with a caramel topping.

Flor de izote   yuca flower used in Salvadoran cooking.

Frijoles volteados   Guatemalan thick refried beans.

Frutería   fruit and vegetable store.

Fugaza   Argentinean flat bread.

Gallo en chicha   festive Salvadoran dish of chicken stewed in **chicha** (fermented drink).

Gallo pinto   Costa Rican and Nicaraguan rice and beans.

Gandules   pigeon peas, also known as *guandu*.

Garbanzos   chickpeas.

Gorditas   small fat tortillas with different fillings.

Guacho   soupy rice.

Guaguas de pan   Ecuadorian bread dolls made for the celebration of the Day of the Dead.

Guajillos   dried chiles used to make salsas and **moles**.

Guanábana   soursop.

Guanimes de maíz   Dominican cornmeal tamales with meat filling; Puerto Rican cornmeal tamales made with coconut milk and molasses.

Guaques   Guatemalan chiles.

Guaraná   Brazilian fruit with high caffeine content used to make drinks and colas.

Guascas   Colombian herb used to flavor **ajiaco** (chicken, maize, and potato stew).

Habaneros   very hot chiles.

Habichuelas con dulce   Dominican dessert of pureed red kidney beans cooked with milk and coconut milk, sweet potatoes, raisins, sugar, and spices.

Hallacas   *(hayacas)* Venezuelan tamales.

Hojaldras   puff pastry.

Horchata   ground rice and almond beverage, flavored with cinnamon.

Huacatay   *(wacataya)* Andean herb sometimes called "black mint."

Humitas   *(humintas)* fresh maize tamales.

Indio viejo   Nicaraguan shredded beef dish.

Jalapeños   medium hot green chiles.

Jamaica   hibiscus flower.

Jícama   root vegetable of white crispy flesh.

Jocote   tropical fruit, also known as *ciruela* or hog plum.

Llajua   Bolivian table condiment made with *rocoto* peppers and *quilquiña* (Bolivian herb).

Llapingachos   Ecuadorian potato and cheese patties.

Locrio   Dominican rice, meat, and vegetable dishes.

Locro   Andean potato-based, cream-style soup; in the Southern Cone, it refers to hominy soups.

Longaniza   pork sausage.

Loroco   edible flower buds used in Salvadoran cooking.

Lulo   tropical fruit, also known as *naranjilla*.

Maduros   fried ripe plantain slices, also known as *tajadas*.

Majarete   Caribbean maize and coconut milk pudding.

Malagueta   Brazilian hot chile; in Spanish, it also refers to allspice.

Malanga   underground stem of a plant of the genus Xanthosoma.

Mamey   fruit of fragrant and bright orange flesh, also known as *mamey sapote*.

Mangú   Dominican mashed plantain dish.

Marquesote   sponge cake.

Marqueta   (*marketa*) market in Spanish Harlem.

Masa   dough; in Mexican cooking, it refers to dough made with nixtamalized maize.

Masa harina   instant dried nixtamalized maize dough.

Matambre   Argentine rolled flank steak with vegetable and egg filling.

Mate   stimulant infusion made with *yerba mate* leaves that is popular in South America.

Mazamorra   generic name of dishes with a mushy consistency.

Medialuna   Argentine croissant-shaped pastry.

Membrillo   quince fruit.

Menudo   Mexican tripe stew.

Mercado   market.

Milanesa   breaded steak.

Mofongo   Puerto Rican ground fried green plantain dish.

Mojito   Cuban rum, mint, and lime cocktail.

Mojito isleño   Puerto Rican tomato and onion sauce used for fish and as dip for fritters.

Mojo   Cuban citrus and garlic marinade.

Molcajete   Mexican lava stone mortar and pestle.

Mole   wide variety of complex Mexican sauces made with ground chiles and spices.

Mole poblano   well-known variety of *mole* that contains chocolate, among many other ingredients.

Molinillo   Mexican whisk used to froth chocolate drinks.

Molino   rotary grinder.

Mondongo   tripe stew.

Moqueca   Brazilian stews flavored with *dendê oil.*

Morcilla   blood sausage.

Morir soñando   Dominican orange juice and evaporated milk shake.

Moros y cristianos   Cuban rice and black beans.

Mote   hominy.

Mote con huesillos   Chilean dessert made with cooked wheat berries and dried peaches.

Mulatos   dried chiles used to make salsas and *moles.*

Nacatamales   Nicaraguan *tamales.*

Ñames   root vegetable used in Caribbean cooking.

Nance   round orange-yellow fruit used in beverages.

Nixtamalization   boiling and soaking dried maize kernels in a slaked lime solution.

Nopalitos   tender pads of the prickly pear cactus.

Olla   generic name for pot; Mexican unglazed earthenware pot.

Pabellón criollo   Venezuelan platter containing rice, shredded beef, and black beans.

Pacaya   tender palm tree blossoms used in Central American cooking.

Paella   saffron-flavored rice dish with seafood, poultry, and/or meat.

Palmitos   hearts of palm.

Pamplona   Uruguayan stuffed, pounded meat or chicken.

Pan cubano   Cuban bread made with lard or vegetable shortening.

Pan de coco   coconut bread popular in Honduras.

Pan de muerto   egg-rich bread made for the celebration of the Mexican Day of the Dead.

Pan de yemas   egg-rich bread.

Pan dulce   sweet bread rolls.

Panadería   bakery.

Pandebono   Colombian cheese and **yuca** starch bread.

Pão de queijo   Brazilian cheese and **yuca** breads.

Parihuela   Peruvian seafood soup.

Parrillada   mixed grilled meats.

Pasilla   dry chile used to make salsas and *moles.*

Pasta frola   Argentinean fruit tarts.

Pastel de choclo   Chilean pot pie made with chicken or beef with a sweet fresh maize topping.

Pastel tres leches   three milk cake.

Pasteles   Puerto Rican tamales made with plantains, root vegetables, and pork.

Pastelitos   sweet or savory pastries, also known as *pastelillos.*

Pastelón   layered casseroles.

Pebre   Chilean hot cilantro table condiment.

Pegao   crispy rice that sticks to the bottom of the pot, also known as *concón.*

Pescadería   fish shop.

Picadillo   seasoned ground meat dish; Costa Rican minced vegetable dishes.

Pilón   Caribbean mortar and pestle traditionally made of wood.

Piloncillo   unrefined cane sugar, also known as *chancaca* and *panela.*

Piña colada   Caribbean rum, pineapple, and coconut cream cocktail.

Pipián   (*pepián*) Mayan dish of meat or chicken and vegetables in ground seeds and nuts sauce.

Piraguas   shaved ice with syrup, also known as *frío frío,nieves*, and *raspados.*

Pisco   brandy produced in Chile and Perú.

Poblanos   large fleshy chiles used to make *chiles rellenos* (stuffed chiles).

Ponche   punch.

Pozole   (*posole*) hominy; hominy stew.

Pulpeta   Cuban meatloaf.

Pupusas   Salvadoran stuffed maize tortillas.

Quelites   lamb's quarters.

Quesadillas   Mexican cheese-filled maize tortillas; Central American cheesecakes.

Queso blanco   generic name for a variety of Latin American fresh cheeses.

Quilquiña   (*quirquiña*) Bolivian herb used in salsas and salads.

Quipes   (*kipes*) Dominican *kibbeh* (bulgur and meat fritters).

Recao   long leaf cilantro, also known as *culantro.*

Refajo   Colombian drink of mixed beer and cola champagne.

Rellenos de papa   meat-stuffed potato croquettes, also known as *papas rellenas.*

Repostería   cake and pastry shop.

Rocoto (locoto)   thick-walled hot peppers used in Bolivian and Peruvian cooking for stuffing and as a seasoning.

Rompope   Mexican eggnog.

Ropa vieja   Cuban shredded beef dish.

Rosca de reyes   Mexican ring-shaped sweet bread made for Three Kings Day.

Salchichón   cured pork sausage.

Salpicón de frutas   Colombian beverage made with chopped fresh fruits and soda.

Salteñas   Bolivian meat turnovers.

Sancocho   thick stew made with a variety of meats and vegetables.

Sangría   wine punch with fresh chopped fruit.

Sangrita   spicy tequila chaser made with tomato and orange juice.

Semita   Mexican sweet bread rolls; Salvadoran flat sweet bread with fruit filling.

Silpancho   Bolivian dish of breaded steak, rice, fried potatoes, fried egg, and salad.

Sofrito   ground paste made with onion, garlic, peppers, and herbs used as a flavor base for many dishes.

Sopaipillas   fried puff pastry or tortilla pieces.

Sopes   small baskets of nixtamalized maize dough with a variety of savory fillings and garnishes.

Sorullitos   Puerto Rican cornmeal sticks.

Tamarillo   Andean fruit used in juices and shakes, also known as *tomate de árbol* (tree tomato).

Taquería   taco shop.

Tasajo   salt dried beef.

Tequeños   Venezuelan cheese pastries.

Tequila   Mexican spirit made from blue agave.

Tomatillo   husk tomato, also known as *miltomate*.

Torrejas   dessert similar to French toast.

Tortilla   in Central America and Mexico, it refers to maize or wheat flat breads; in the Caribbean and South America, it means omelette.

Tortillería   tortilla shop.

Tostado   Andean toasted maize.

Tostones   twice-fried thick green plantain slices, also known as *patacones* and *tachinos*.

Tuna   prickly pear, fruit of the *nopal* cactus.

Vatapá   Brazilian condiment made with ground dried shrimp, coconut milk, **dendê oil,** and cashews or peanuts.

Verdolagas   purslane.

Vigorón   Nicaraguan dish of yuca, *chicharrón* (fried pork rind), and salad.

Vivero   live poultry shop.

Yaniqueques   Dominican fried flat bread.

Yautía   underground stem of a plant of the genus Xanthosoma of different varieties.

Yuca   *(yucca)* cassava.

Zapallo   Andean pumpkin.

Resource Guide

COOKBOOKS

Baez Kijac, Maria. *The South American Table: The Flavor and Soul of Authentic Home Cooking from Patagonia to Rio de Janeiro, with 450 Recipes.* Boston: Harvard Common Press, 2003.

Beatriz, María Dolores. *Latina Lite Cooking: 200 Delicious Lowfat Recipes from All over the Americas.* New York: Warner, 1998.

Behnke, Alison. *Cooking the Central American Way.* Minneapolis: Lerner, 2005.

Bodega de la familia. *La cocina de la familia: Las recetas de Alphabet City: Un vecindario celebra el lenguaje común de la comida.* New York: La bodega de la familia, 1998.

Buia, Carolina, and Isabel González. *Latin Chic: Entertaining with Style and Sass.* New York: Rayo, 2005.

Cordero-Cordell, Teresa, and Robert Cordell. *Aprovecho: A Mexican American Border Cookbook.* New York: Hippocrene, 2007.

Creen, Linette, and Felipe Rojas-Lombardi. *A Taste of Cuba: Recipes from the Cuban American Community.* New York: Dutton, 1991.

Delgado, Abel. *Curas de la cocina latina: Desde el aguacate hasta la yuca, la guía máxima del poder curativo de la nutrición.* Emmaus, Pa.: Rodale Press, 1999.

Hermalyn, Gary, and Peter Derrick. *The Bronx Cookbook.* Bronx, N.Y.: The Society, 1997.

Jamison, Cheryl Alters. *The Border Cookbook: Authentic Home Cooking of the American Southwest and Northern Mexico.* Boston: Harvard Common Press, 1995.

Kennedy, Diana. *The Cuisines of Mexico.* New York: Harper & Row, 1972.

Martínez, Daisy. *Daisy Cooks! Latin Flavors That Will Rock Your World.* New York: Hyperion, 2005.

Ortiz, Yvonne. *A Taste of Puerto Rico: Traditional and New Dishes from the Puerto Rican Community*. New York: Dutton, 1994.

Palomino, Rafael. *Viva la Vida: Festive Recipes for Entertaining Latin-Style*. San Francisco: Chronicle, 2002.

Raichlen, Steven. *Steven Raichlen's Healthy Latin Cooking: 200 Sizzling Recipes from Mexico, Cuba, Caribbean, Brazil and Beyond*. Emmaus, Pa.: Rodale Press, 1998.

Rexach, Nilda Luz. *The Hispanic Cookbook: Traditional and Modern Recipes in English and Spanish*. Secaucus, N.J.: Carol Publishing, 1995.

Rivera, Oswald. *Puerto Rican Cuisine in America: Nuyorican and Bodega Recipes*. New York: Four Walls Eight Windows, 1993.

Rodríguez, Douglas. *Nuevo Latino: Recipes That Celebrate the New Latin-American Cuisine*. Berkeley: Ten Speed Press, 1995.

———. *Douglas Rodríguez's Latin Flavors on the Grill*. Berkeley: Ten Speed Press, 2000.

———. *The Great Ceviche Book*. Berkeley: Ten Speed Press, 2003.

Sánchez, Aarón. *La comida del barrio: Latin-American Cooking in the U.S.A.* New York: Clarkson Potter, 2003.

Saralegui, Fernando. *Our Latin Table: Celebrations, Recipes and Memories*. Boston: Bulfinch Press, 2003.

Stallworth, Lyn, and Rod Kennedy Jr. *The Brooklyn Cookbook*. New York: Knopf, 1991.

Tapp, Alice Guadalupe. *Tamales 101: A Beginner's Guide to Making Traditional Tamales*. Berkeley: Ten Speed Press, 2002.

Tausend, Marilyn, and Miguel Ravago. *Cocina de la familia: More Than 200 Authentic Recipes from Mexican American Home Kitchens*. New York: Simon & Schuster, 1997.

Women's Collaborative for Health and Nutrition. *Sabores de Mexico: A Community Cookbook*. Plumas County, Calif.: Sierra Institute, 2007.

GROCERY AND RESTAURANT GUIDES

Bladholm, Linda. *Latin & Caribbean Grocery Stores Demystified*. Los Angeles: Renaissance, 2001.

González, Carolina, and Seth Kugel. *Nueva York: The Complete Guide to Latino Life in the Five Boroughs*. New York: St. Martin's Griffin, 2006.

Parker, Suzanne. *Eating Like Queens: A Guide to Ethnic Dining in America's Melting Pot, Queens, New York*. Madison, Wis.: Jones Brooks, 2005.

WEB SITES

http://www.carnegielibrary.org/subject/food/latin.html (Collection of Latin American food and cooking links by the Carnegie Library of Pittsburgh)

http://lanic.utexas.edu/la/region/food/ (Portal on Latin American food, recipes, and
nutrition by the Latin American Network Information Center)

http://latino.si.edu/education/education_foodways.htm (Latino foodways page by the
Smithsonian Latino Center)

http://www.public.iastate.edu/~savega/us_latin.htm (Collections of links to U.S. Latino Web sites kept by Iowa State University)

Bibliography

Abarca, Meredith E. *Voices in the Kitchen: Views of Food and the World from Working-Class Mexican and Mexican American Women*. College Station: Texas A&M University Press, 2006.

Arias, Arturo. "Central American-Americans? Re-mapping Latino/Latin American Subjectivities on Both Sides of the Great Divide (Social, Cultural Presence, Influences, of Central Americans in the United States)." *Explicación de Textos Literarios* 47, no. 17 (Winter–Summer 1999): 47–48.

Arreola, Daniel D. "Hispanic American Legacy, Latino American Diaspora." In *Hispanic Spaces, Latino Places: Community and Cultural Diversity in Contemporary America*, ed. Daniel D. Arreola, pp. 13–35. Austin: University of Texas Press, 2004.

Arreola, Daniel D. *Tejano South Texas: A Mexican American Cultural Province*. Austin: University of Texas Press, 2002.

Bellows, Anne C. "Oaxacan Women in New Jersey and Mexico: Family Health in the Context of Migration and Changing Food Environments." Paper presented at the 20th Joint Annual Meeting of the Agriculture, Food and Human Values Society and the Association for the Study of Food and Society. Victoria, B.C., Canada. June 2006.

Bentley, Amy. "From Culinary Other to Mainstream America: Meanings and Uses of Southwestern Cuisine." In *Culinary Tourism*, ed. Lucy M. Long, pp. 209–25. Lexington: University Press of Kentucky, 2004.

Beserra, Bernadete. "From Brazilians to Latinos? Racialization and Latinidad in the Making of Brazilian Carnival in Los Angeles." *Latino Studies* 3, no. 1 (Autumn 2005): 53–75.

Boswell, Thomas D. *The Cuban-American Experience: Culture, Images and Perspectives*. Totowa, N.J.: Rowman & Allanheld, 1984.

Bowen, Dana. "Street Corner Cooks Have Names, Too." *New York Times*, September 22, 2004.

Campa, Arthur L. *Hispanic Culture in the Southwest*. Norman: University of Oklahoma Press, 1979.

Cason, Katherine, et al. "Dietary Intake and Food Security among Migrant Farm Workers in Pennsylvania." *Harris School Working Paper Series* 4, no. 2 (November 2003).

Coe, Sophie D. *America's First Cuisines*. Austin: University of Texas Press, 1994.

Cordova, Carlos B. *The Salvadoran Americans*. Westport, Conn.: Greenwood Press, 2005.

De la Torre, Miguel A. *Santería: The Beliefs and Rituals of a Growing Religion in America*. Grand Rapids, Mich.: William B. Eerdmans, 2004.

Denker, Joel. *The World on a Plate: A Tour through the History of America's Ethnic Cuisines*. Boulder, Colo.: Westview Press, 2003.

Duany, Jorge. *The Puerto Rican Nation on the Move: Identities on the Island and in the United States*. Chapel Hill: University of North Carolina Press, 2002.

Gabaccia, Donna R. *We Are What We Eat: Ethnic Food and the Making of Americans*. Cambridge, Mass.: Harvard University Press, 1998.

García, María Cristina. *Havana USA: Cuban Exiles and Cuban-Americans in South Florida, 1959–1994*. Berkeley: University of California Press, 1996.

Grosfoguel, Ramón and Chloé S. Geroas. "Latino Caribbean Diasporas in New York." In *Mambo Montage: The Latinization of New York*, ed. Agustín Laó-Montes and Arlene Dávila, pp. 97–118. New York: Columbia University Press, 2001.

Janer, Zilkia. "(In)Edible Nature: New World Food and Coloniality." *Cultural Studies* 21, nos. 2–3 (March/May 2007): 402–403.

Knauer, Lisa Maya. "Eating in Cuban." In *Mambo Montage: The Latinization of New York*, ed. Agustín Laó-Montes and Arlene Dávila, pp. 425–47. New York: Columbia University Press, 2001.

Long-Solís, Janet, and Luis Alberto Vargas. *Food Culture in Mexico*. Westport, Conn.: Greenwood Press, 2005.

Lovera, José Rafael. *Gastronomía caribeña: Historia, recetas y bibliografía*. Caracas: CEGA, 1991.

Mahler, Sarah J. *Salvadorans in Suburbia: Symbiosis and Conflict*. Boston: Allyn and Bacon, 1995.

Melero Malpica, Daniel. "Indigenous Mexican Migrants in a Modern Metropolis: The Reconstruction of Latino Communities in Los Angeles." In *Latino Los Angeles: Transformations, Communities, and Activism*, ed. Enrique C. Ochoa and Gilda L. Ochoa, pp. 111–36. Tucson: University of Arizona Press, 2005.

Menard, Valerie. *The Latino Holiday Book: From Cinco de Mayo to Dia de los Muertos: The Celebrations and Traditions of Hispanic-Americans*. New York: Marlowe and Co., 2000.

Miles, Ann. *From Cuenca to Queens: An Anthropological Story of Transnational Migration*. Austin: University of Texas Press, 2004.

Miyares, Inés M. "Changing Latinization of New York City." In *Hispanic Spaces, Latino Places: Community and Cultural Diversity in Contemporary America*, ed. Daniel D. Arreola, pp. 145–66. Austin: University of Texas Press, 2004.

Montaño, Mario. "Appropriation and Counterhegemony in South Texas: Food Slurs, Offal Meats, and Blood." In *Usable Pasts: Traditions and Group Expressions in North America,* ed. Tad Tuleja, pp. 50–67. Logan: Utah State University Press, 1997.

Ochoa, Enrique C., and Gilda L. Ochoa, eds. *Latino Los Angeles: Transformations, Communities, and Activism.* Tucson: University of Arizona Press, 2005.

Pilcher, Jeffrey M. "Tex-Mex, Cal-Mex, New Mex, or Whose Mex? Notes on the Historical Geography of Southwestern Cuisine." *Journal of the Southwest* 43, no. 4 (Winter 2001): 659–680.

Price, Cindy. "Chasing the Perfect Taco up the California Coast." *New York Times,* July 21, 2006.

Ricourt, Milagros. *Hispanas de Queens: Latino Panethnicity in a New York City Neighborhood.* Ithaca, N.Y.: Cornell University Press, 2003.

Rodríguez, Ana Patricia. "'Departamento 15': Cultural Narratives of Salvadoran Transnational Migration." *Latino Studies* 3, no. 1 (Spring 2005): 19–41.

Sahagún, Bernardino de. *General History of the Things of New Spain.* Book 8: "Kings and Lords." Santa Fe, N.M.: School of American Research, 1953–82.

Sahagún, Bernardino de. *General History of the Things of New Spain.* Book 10: "The People." Santa Fe, N.M.: School of American Research, 1953–82.

Sánchez, Rosaura. *Telling Identities: The Californio Testimonios.* Berkeley: University of California Press, 1995.

Smith, Robert C. *Mexican New York: Transnational Lives of New Immigrants.* Berkeley: University of California Press, 2006.

Strehl, Dan, ed. and trans. *Encarnación's Kitchen: Mexican Recipes from Nineteenth-Century California.* Berkeley: University of California Press, 2003.

Trotter, Robert. *Curanderismo: Mexican American Folk Healing.* Athens: University of Georgia Press, 1981.

Valle, Víctor M. "A Curse of Tea and Potatoes: The Life and Recipes of Encarnación Pinedo." In *Encarnación's Kitchen: Mexican Recipes from Nineteenth-Century California,* ed. and trans. Dan Strehl, pp. 1–17. Berkeley: University of California Press, 2003.

Valle, Víctor M. *Recipe of Memory: Five Generations of Mexican Cuisine.* New York: New Press, 1995.

Valle, Víctor M., and Rodolfo D. Torres. *Latino Metropolis.* Minneapolis: University of Minnesota Press, 2000.

Walsh, Robb. *Tex-Mex: A History in Recipes and Photos.* New York: Broadway, 2004.

Williams, Brett. "Why Migrant Women Feed Their Husbands Tamales: Foodways as a Basis for a Revisionist View of Tejano Family Life." In *Ethnic and Regional Foodways in the United States: The Performance of Group Identity,* ed. Linda Keller Brown and Kay Mussell, pp. 113–26. Knoxville: University of Tennessee Press, 1984.

Index

About the Author

ZILKIA JANER teaches Latin American and Latino literature and culture at Hofstra University. She is the author of *Puerto Rican Nation-Building Literature: Impossible Romance* (2005) and has published a number of articles on Latin American and South Asian culinary cultures.